MALAYSIA

How to use our guide

These 192 pages cover the **highlights** of Malaysia, grouped by region. Although not exhaustive, our selection of sights will enable you to make the best of your trip.

 Places of interest are described between pages 54 and 146. Those most highly recommended are flagged by the Berlitz tick.

The **Where to Go** section on pages 51–3 will help you plan your visit according to the time available.

For **general background** see the sections Malaysia: the Country and the People (p10) and History (p16).

Entertainment and **activities** (including eating out) are found on pages 147–67.

The **practical information**, hints and tips you will need before and during your trip begin on page 168.

The **maps** on the flaps and inside the book will help you find your way around and locate the principal sights.

Finally, if there is anything you cannot find, refer to the **index** (pp190–2).

CONTENTS

CONTENTS

Text:	Jack Altman
Staff editor:	Delphine Verroest
Layout:	Suzanna Boyle
Photography:	All photographs by Lam Seng Fatt, except those on pages 17, 21, 28–9, 31, 42–3, 50, 54–5, 66–7, 70, 71, 73, 76, 94–5, 100, 102, 115, 118–19, 123, 129, 132–3, 134–5, 150 and 162 by Jack Altman, and on pages 23, 142, 143 and 145 by Walter Imber
Cartography:	MicroMap, Romsey, Hampshire

Acknowledgements
We would like to thank the Malaysian Tourist Development Corporation (UK) and Lam Seng Fatt for their help in the preparation of this guide.

Found an error or an omission in this Berlitz guide? Or a change or new feature we should know about? Our editor would be happy to hear from you. Write to: Berlitz Publishing Company Ltd., Berlitz House, Peterley Road, Oxford OX4 2TX, England.

Although we have made every effort to ensure the accuracy of all the information in this book, changes occur incessantly. We cannot therefore take responsibility for facts, prices, addresses and circumstances in general that are constantly subject to alteration.

Cover: *front* Wat Chayamangkalaram Buddhist monastery, Penang (Tony Stone Worldwide); *back* Tea plantation in the Cameron Highlands (Lam Seng Fatt).

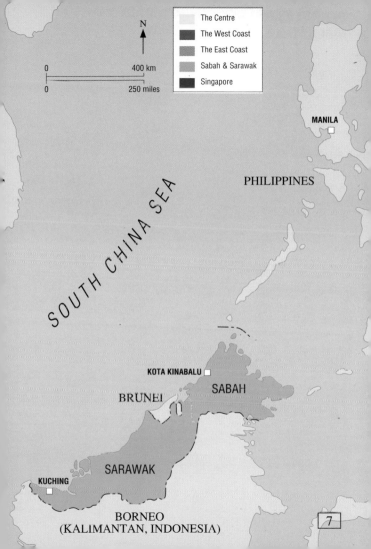

	The Centre
	The West Coast
	The East Coast
	Sabah & Sarawak
	Singapore

N

0   400 km

0   250 miles

MANILA □

PHILIPPINES

SOUTH CHINA SEA

KOTA KINABALU □

BRUNEI

SABAH

SARAWAK

KUCHING □

BORNEO
(KALIMANTAN, INDONESIA)

7

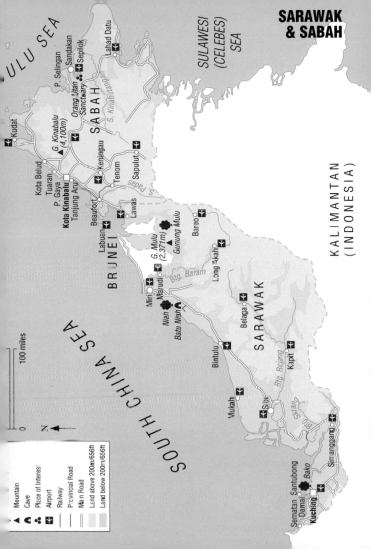

MALAYSIA: THE COUNTRY AND THE PEOPLE

The only head hunters you will find in the jungles of Borneo these days are the ones on vacation from management consultancy jobs in the national capital, Kuala Lumpur. But if Malaysians have moved resolutely into the modern age, they have not lost all contact with more traditional values—hence its fascinating culture. Luckily for the visitor, Malaysia offers the best of both worlds: the creature comforts inherent in an affluent country, as well as the untamed wilderness of its tropical rainforests.

With Thailand to its north, peninsular Malaysia forms a natural bridge between Asia's continental land mass and the archipelago of Indonesia. Since the warm-up after the last Ice Age, a broad channel of the South China Sea separates the peninsula from East Malaysia, on the north coast of Borneo. (The country adopted the name of Malaysia in 1963 to replace the pre-Independence 'Malaya'.)

The divided territories—with a total land surface larger than New Mexico and almost as large as Germany—have in common their hot humid climate but differ greatly in population density. Industry and urban population are concentrated on the peninsula, particularly along the west coast, while East Malaysia is dominated inland by the country's characteristic impenetrable jungle.

This is a prosperous country with an excellent network of roads and a good railway along the peninsula's west coast. Per capita income is second in South-East Asia only to neighbouring Singapore. Some 40 per cent of Malaysians live in townships of more than 5,000 inhabitants—an exceptional proportion for the region. Its mortality rate of 7 per 1,000 is one of the lowest in the world. Nobody has suffered grave enough hardships to give revolution here a serious possibility of success.

Kuala Lumpur, the capital of Malaysia, marches resolutely towards the future— as do its people.

Nature's Supremacy

Whether you are staying at beach resorts or visiting the cities, you will always find the jungle ready to re-assert its rights. In Kuala Lumpur—as modern an urban sprawl as you could imagine, criss-crossed by ex-pressways and bristling with sky-scrapers—a construction site aban-doned a moment too long to the tropical sun and rain will soon sprout a luxuriant growth of *lallang* ferns and wild creepers.

Over the centuries, the country's prosperity has come from its coastal plains, wider on the west than the east side of the peninsula. Malaysia rose first as a trading point for Asia and Europe, with the ports of Melaka (Malacca in colonial times) and later Singapore, now sovereign and independent. Then came tin mining and rubber plantations and, more recently, palm oil, hardwood timber, offshore petroleum and gas. Rice paddies in the north-west to-wards the Thai border and around river deltas on the east coast serve only domestic consumption.

Mangrove swamps, found in coastal areas, and squat nipa palms give rise to mangrove jungle.

Malaysia offers unspoilt natural beauties, such as this beach on Pulau Sapi, and an unaffected lifestyle.

Untouched by the Ice Age, the world's oldest rainforests engulf low but steeply rising mountain chains which cross the peninsula from east to west like ribs, with one long north–south Main Range as their backbone. Until the highway construction of the modern era, access to the jungle interior has been—and in some cases still is—only by river.

The beds are mostly too shallow for anything but flat-bottomed boats, drawing aboriginal communities to settle along the banks.

On the great island of Borneo, East Malaysia's States of Sarawak and Sabah surround the enclave of the oil-rich sultanate of Brunei. Plantations alternate with marshland on the coastal plain before giving way to the all-powerful jungle of the interior. Navigation is hindered by sand-bars at the mouth and rapids upriver, though small sea-going vessels can make fair headway up the Rejang in Sarawak and up

13

the Kinabatangan in Sabah. To the south, a natural barrier of mountain ranges constitutes the border with Indonesian Kalimantan. Near the coast at the northern end of the Crocker Range is Mount Kinabalu, at 4,100m (13,450ft) the highest peak in South-East Asia and a favourite with climbers, both professional and amateur.

With the growth of tourism as a major industry, resort facilities have burgeoned in smaller islands such as Penang, Pangkor and Langkawi on the west coast of the peninsula, Tioman on the east coast, and around Sabah's offshore nature reserve near Kota Kinabalu.

Top of a Quiet World

In an era of seemingly perpetual ethnic hostilities, Malaysia can be proud of a unique achievement—the coexistence of the three most prominent peoples of Asia: Malays (mostly Muslim), Chinese and Indians. Despite occasional conflicts, they live in a remarkable state of harmony, avoiding most of the violence that characterizes other mixed societies around the world. It is not unusual to find, as in old Melaka, Buddhist and Hindu temples on the same street as a mosque. Not least of all, it makes for a marvellous diversity in national cuisines, with food-centres often serving Malay, Chinese and Indian dishes at adjacent stalls (see pp163–7).

With Islam as the national religion and Malay—*Bahasa Malaysia*—as the national language, Malays enjoy practically exclusive access to the principal positions of government at federal and state level. They share a common ancestry with inhabitants of the Indonesian archipelago. At the upper end of the social scale, Malays make up the royal courts of the sultanates—country gentry enjoying an occasional game of polo and the other good things of life. Further down, urban Malays form a modern bourgeoisie, cultivating contacts with the Arab Middle East and keeping only a remote eye on their country estates. The more prosperous send their children to British schools.

But the bulk of Malays in the country at large are humbler village-dwelling peasants—herding goats and buffaloes, growing rice, working in the coconut, rubber, timber, rattan, and bamboo industries. Just as court ritual is still coloured by the ancient customs of pre-Muslim Malaya, so a mild-mannered Sunnite version of the Muslim religion is often seasoned, amid this all-pervasive nature, with a generous spoonful of the more ancient beliefs of animist medicine-men.

The Malays have a perfect understanding of their tropical climate. They know how important it is to keep cool and calm and move around slowly. Their relaxed attitude to life is delightfully infectious to the newcomer, who soon learns to shrug off the stresses of more hustling civilizations.

FACTS & FIGURES

Geography: Peninsular and East Malaysia together cover a total land surface of 329,759sq km (127,317sq miles). From the Thai border to the causeway across to Singapore island, the peninsula is 750km (470 miles) long and about 350km (218 miles) at its widest point. It is only two-thirds the size of East Malaysia, which stretches along the north Borneo coast, embracing the enclave of the the Brunei sultanate and bordering on Indonesian Kalimantan to the south. Some four-fifths of Malaysia are covered by rainforest. Of the countless rivers that crisscross the land, the peninsula's longest are the Pahang, with 475km (297 miles) and the Perak, with 400km (250 miles). In East Malaysia, the longest river is the Rejang, with 563km (350 miles). On the peninsula, the mountains of the central Main Range rise from 900m. (nearly 3,000ft) to 2,000m (6,500ft), the tallest being Mount Tahan in the eastern highlands, at 2,187m (7,186ft). But the country's highest peak, indeed the highest in South-East Asia, is in East Malaysia: Mount Kinabalu, at 4,100m (13,450ft).

Population: 18,257,300, of which 59% are Malays and other bumiputra (aborigines), 32% of Chinese origin and 8% from the Indian subcontinent.

Capital: Kuala Lumpur 1,191,630.

Major Cities: Ipoh 380,769; Georgetown 321,670; Johor Bahru 319,278; Petaling Jaya 269,273; Klang, 248,897; Kuala Terengganu 233,627; Kota Bharu 217,528.

Government: The independent nation was founded in 1963 as a federation of 14 states. The state rulers are known variously as Sultan, Raja and Governor. In a unique form of rotating constitutional monarchy, nine of the rulers choose from among themselves a Supreme Head of State, who is elected for five years. Government is in the hands of a prime minister and a cabinet appointed from a 180-member House of Representatives, democratically elected for a maximum of five years. An advisory Senate consisting of 68 members serves a three year term. State legislatures administer local land affairs and govern Islamic, personal and family law.

Religion: Muslim 53%; Buddhist 17%; Confucian and Taoist 12%; Christian 9%; Hindu 7%; Folk/Tribal 2%.

HISTORY

Over the centuries, the living here has always been easy enough to attract a steady stream of immigrants. Bountiful edible plants and animals in the rainforests, and fish in the rivers and surrounding seas must have made Malaysia an inviting habitation for the contemporaries of Java Man—230 000 BC. But thus far, the country's earliest traces of *homo sapiens*, found in the Niah Caves of northern Sarawak, are fragments of a skull dating back to 40 000 BC.

On the peninsula, the oldest human-related relics (10 000 BC) are Stone Age tools of the Negritos. These small dark Melanesians are related in type to Australian aborigines and are confined today to the forests of the northern highlands.

By 2000 BC, these timid, gentle nomads hunting with bow and arrow were driven back from the coasts by waves of sturdy immigrants arriving in outrigger canoes equipped with sails. Mongolians from South China and Polynesians and Malay peoples from the Philippines and the Indonesian islands settled along the rivers of the peninsula and northern Borneo. They practised a slash-and-burn agriculture of yams and millet, a technique that exhausted the soil and imposed a semi-nomadic existence from one jungle clearing to another. Families lived in wooden longhouses like those still to be seen today among the Iban peoples of Sarawak. Another unit was added on to the communal dwelling each time a marriage created a new family.

Other tough migrants from the South Seas settled along the coasts—sailors, fishermen, traders—for the most part pirates—known euphemistically as *orang laut* (sea people).

Indian Influence

In the early centuries of the Christian era, the peninsula's advantageous position made it an ideal way station for trade with Bengal and southern India and attracted Indianized colonies from the Mekong valley of Indochina. Their rulers introduced Buddhist and Hindu culture, Brahmin ministers to govern and an elaborate court ritual.

What is now the northern State of Kedah benefited from the plough and other Indian farming practices. An Indian traveller described the prosperous Bujang Valley settlement as 'the seat of all felicities'. From its golden era, a 9th-century Hindu temple, the Candi Bukit Batu Pahat, has been restored on the southern slopes of Mount Jerai. On the east coast in Terengganu and Kelantan, the weaving and metalwork still practised today trace their origins to this early colonization. So do the region's *wayang kulit* shadow plays inspired by the dramas of the ancient Indian epics, *Ramayana* and *Mahabharata* (see pp154–5).

Srivijaya, most powerful of the Indianized colonies and a centre of Buddhist learning, built a maritime empire from its base on the island of

The Malay Sultanate Palace, in Melaka, exhibits the splendour of the sultans' regalia.

Sumatra. With the *orang laut* pirates as allies, Srivijaya controlled the Straits of Melaka (known in colonial times as Malacca), key link between the Indian Ocean and the South China Sea. Its colonies on the peninsula's west coast brought with them the Malay language (Malayu was the name of a State on Sumatra).

As Srivijaya declined in the 14th century, the Malay peninsula was carved up among Cambodia, Thailand and the Javanese Hindu empire of Majapahit. Around the year 1400, fighting over the island of Singapore drove the Srivijaya prince Parameswara to seek refuge up the peninsula coast with his *orang laut* pirate friends in their small fishing village of Melaka.

The Glory of Melaka

In the early days, if you were not a pirate or a mosquito, Melaka was not much of a place to live in. The land was infertile, just a swampy plain, the river small and sluggish. But it had a sheltered harbour, protected from the monsoons by neighbouring Sumatra.

Initially, it attracted only fishing and petty trade. Later, the strategic location and deep-water channel close to the coast brought in the bigger vessels of the trade wind traffic crossing the Indian Ocean. The

17

Dog Day Afternoon
According to Malay legend, Prince Parameswara was awakened from his afternoon siesta by the yelping of one of his hunting dogs. The runt had, justifiably, been kicked by a mouse-deer he had been harassing. For some reason, this was considered to be an omen of good luck, so the prince decided to found his new kingdom on the spot and named it after the tree under which he been sleeping—a malaka *tree. Far fetched? Would you prefer the more boring and, no doubt, more correct explanation of the town's name, after a nearby island known by an Arab word for market—*malakat?

---

first to realize the larger commercial potential, as so often throughout the country's subsequent history, were the Chinese.

In 1409, under a new directive from Emperor Chu Ti to pursue trade in the South Seas and the Indian Ocean, a Chinese fleet of 50 ships headed by Admiral Cheng Ho called in at Melaka. They made Parameswara an offer he could not refuse: port facilities and an annual financial tribute in exchange for Chinese protection against the marauding Thais. In 1411, Parameswara took the money to Peking himself and the emperor gratefully made him a vassal king.

Twenty years later, the Chinese withdrew again from the South Seas trade. The new ruler of Melaka, Sri Maharajah, switched his allegiance to the Muslim trading fraternity by marrying into the Muslim faith, wedding the daughter of a sultan in Sumatra.

Islam won its place in Malaya not by conquest—as had been the case in North Africa or Europe—but by trade, dynastic alliances and peaceful preaching. Bengali pedlars had already brought the faith to the east coast. In Melaka and throughout the peninsula, Islam thrived as a strong male-dominated religion of individuality, offering dynamic leadership, and preaching brotherhood and self-reliance—all qualities ideally suited to the coastal trade. At the same time, Sufi mystics happily synthesized Islamic teaching with local Malay traditions of animistic magic and charisma.

Although Sri Maharajah took the Muslim name of Mohammed Shah (1424–44), his court remained Hindu in ritual and the nobility retained the Hindu faith. After a couple of years of palace intrigue, his successor Muzaffar Shah became sultan of Melaka (1446–59) and established Islam as the State religion.

But the key figure in the sultanate was Tun Perak, prime minister (*bendahara*) and military commander. He expanded Melaka's power along the west coast and down to Singapore and the neighbouring Bintan islands. He also had *orang laut* pirates patrolling the seas to extort tribute from passing ships. After allied district chiefs had repelled assaults from Thai-controlled armies from Pahang,

Tun Perak personally led a famous victory over a Thai fleet off Batu Pahat in 1456. To smooth things over, the sultan sent a peace mission to the Thai court and, for extra coverage, an envoy to China, reconfirming Muzzafar Shah's title as most obedient vassal.

By 1500, Melaka had become the leading port in South-East Asia, drawing Chinese, Indian, Javanese and Arab merchants away from the hitherto vital port of Pasai in Sumatra. Governed by the great *bendahara* Mutahir with more diplomacy than military force, the sultanate asserted its supremacy over the whole Malay peninsula (except for the northernmost Thai-held Patani region) and across the Melaka Straits to the east coast of Sumatra. Prosperity was based entirely on the entrepôt trade: handling textiles from India, spices from Indonesia, silk and porcelain from China, gold and pepper from Sumatra, camphor from Borneo, sandalwood from Timor, and Malay tin from Perak.

Court life was luxurious, though Islamic scholarship did find a place next to worldly pleasures. The Malay aristocracy preferred to leave commerce to foreigners, principally to Tamil and Gujarati Indians, Javanese and Chinese. Merchant ships often had Malay crews but remained foreign-owned.

The foreign communities lived in four separate districts, each one supervised by a harbour master (*shahbandar*). The four districts consisted of: 1. Gujarati; 2. other Indians and north Sumatrans; 3. people from Java, Borneo, the Philippines, Moluccas and south Sumatra; 4. Chinese and Indochinese. Tamil merchants cultivated the fine arts, music and a gracious style of living. With a fortune equal to the sultan's, the Javanese *shahbandar*, rice-magnate Utimutirajah, lived in a settlement with hundreds of slaves.

Portuguese Conquest

In the 16th century, Melaka fell victim to Portugal's anti-Muslim crusade in the campaign to break the Arab-Venetian domination of commerce between Asia and Europe. A Portuguese ship made its first visit in 1509. Prime Minister Mutahir received these strange 'white Bengalis', as he called them, with customary gifts of precious robes. But Gujarati merchants, embittered by Portuguese hostilities back in India, turned the *bendahara* against them. The captain escaped a murder plot but left 20 of his crew as prisoners. This provided the pretext for Portugal's viceroy in India, Afonso de Albuquerque, to return to Melaka. The real motive was to establish control of the port: a crucial link in Portugal's Asian trading posts between Goa and the Moluccas in Indonesia. Two years after the murder plot, Albuquerque returned with a fleet and seized Melaka.

The Melaka court had been weakened by palace infighting. Resentful of Prime Minister

Mutahir's arrogance, Tamil merchants incited Sultan Mahmud to have him assassinated for treachery. Discovering the charges to be fabricated, Mahmud had the culprits killed or castrated and withdrew into remorseful seclusion. Affairs of State passed to his son, Ahmad, with a frail old man as the new prime minister. They were no match for the Portuguese invaders and the court fled south, establishing a new centre of Malay Muslim power in Johor. The foreign merchants, led by the opportunist Javanese potentate Utimutirajah, made their peace with the conquerors.

Albuquerque built a fortress, which he named *A Famosa* ('The Famous'), and St Paul's church on the site of the sultan's palace. He ruled the non-Portuguese community with Malay *kapitan* headmen and the foreigners' *shahbandar* harbourmasters. Relations were better with Chinese and Indian merchants than with the Muslims. Utimutirajah and his Javanese successor were both executed on conspiracy charges.

The 130 years of Portuguese control proved precarious. They faced repeated assault and siege from neighbouring Malay forces, and malaria was a constant scourge. Unable or unwilling to court the old vassal Malay States or the *orang laut* pirates to patrol the seas, the new rulers forfeited their predecessors' commercial monopoly in the Melaka Straits and, with it, command of the Moluccas spice trade.

They made little effort, despite the Jesuit presence in Asia, to convert local inhabitants to Christianity or to expand their territory into the interior. They hung on for private profit. The original colony of 600 men intermarried with local women to form a large Eurasian community, served by African slaves and living in an elegant luxury that won their trading post the name of 'Babylon of the Orient'.

The Dutch Take Over

Intent on capturing a piece of the Portuguese trade in pepper and other spices, the Java-based Dutch allied with the Malays in the 1633 to blockade Melaka. The trade blockade was to last eight years, and ended in a seven-month siege. The Portuguese surrendered in 1641, wracked by malaria and dysentery and denied their usual reinforcements from Goa. By then, the city they left the Dutch had become a stagnant backwater.

Unlike the Portuguese, the Dutch decided to do business with the Malays of Johor, who controlled the southern half of the peninsula together with Singapore and the neighbouring Riau islands. A trade treaty gave the Dutch command of the spice trade but reserved Johor's rights in tin exports from Perak, Selangor and Klang. Without ever retrieving the supremacy of the old Melaka sultanate, Johor had become the strongest Asian power in the region. For the Dutch, Johor provided a buffer against other Europeans.

Meanwhile, fresh blood came in with the migration into the southern interior of hardy Minangkabau farmers from Sumatra, while tough Bugis warriors from the east Indonesian Celebes (Sulawesi) roved the length and breadth of the peninsula. The Minangkabau custom of freely electing their leaders provided the model for rulership elections in modern federal Malaysia. Their confederation of States became today's Negeri Sembilan ('Nine States'), with Seremban as its capital. The name Minangkabau itself means roughly 'buffalo horns' and is reflected in the distinctive upward curving roof in museums and government offices built in the traditional Minangkabau style.

The Bugis were energetic merchants and great sailors. With the Dutch concentrating once more on Java and the Moluccas in the 18th century, the Bugis took advantage of the vacuum by raiding Perak and Kedah, imposing their chieftains in Selangor and becoming the power behind the throne in Johor. The Bugis in Johor's administration provided much of the spirit in that State's independent stand in the 19th and 20th centuries.

Throughout this period, the east coast States enjoyed a relatively tranquil prosperity, Terengganu notably thriving from its textile industry and trading in pepper and gold with the Thais, Cambodians and Chinese. The British, under the private auspices of the East India Company (EIC), were beginning to poke their noses into North Borneo.

And Then, the British

The first British contacts with Malaya, in the 17th century, had been a few EIC entrepreneurs on the peninsula undercutting the Dutch in the west-coast tin trade. In 1773, testing North Borneo as a base for its China trade, the company set up shop

The Porta de Santiago, in Melaka, is all that's left of the A Famosa fortress, built by Albuquerque in the 16th century.

on Balambangan Island, off the northern tip of present-day Sabah. Although rights had been duly negotiated with the sultan, local warriors burned down the trading post after a year.

The EIC turned back to the Malay peninsula. As a counterweight to the pressing demands of the neighbouring Thais and Burmese, the Sultan of Kedah granted company representative Francis Light, in 1786, rights to the island of Penang and the strip of mainland coast opposite ('Province Wellesley', now Seberang Perai). Unlike Portuguese and Dutch trading posts in the region, Penang was declared a duty-free zone, attracting Malays, Sumatrans, Indians and Chinese to settle and trade. For many merchants, an added lure was Francis Light's decision to import large quantities of opium from India. By 1801, the population was over 10,000, most of them in the island capital Georgetown, thus named in honour of England's future King George IV.

In 1805, a dashing EIC administrator, Thomas Stamford Bingley Raffles, came out to Penang at the age of 24. His knowledge of Malay customs and language, broad-ranging interests in zoology, botany and cartography, as well as a humanitarian vision for the region's future, made him a vital factor in Britain's expanding role in Malay affairs.

Characteristically, while passing through during the British dismantlement of the Melaka trading post and transfer of population to Penang, Raffles halted destruction of the Portuguese *A Famosa* fortress to preserve at least its Santiago gateway. He served as lieutenant-governor in Java and Sumatra, during which time he wrote a *History of Java*. He then secured his own place in history by negotiating with the Sultan of Johor the creation of the Singapore trading post, in 1819. Singapore became the capital of the Straits Settlements—as the EIC called its Malay holdings incorporating Penang and Melaka—and was the linchpin of Britain's 150-year presence in the region.

The Straits Settlements were formed after the Anglo-Dutch Treaty of London (1824). This colonial carve-up partitioned the Malay world through the Melaka Straits. The peninsula and Sumatra, after centuries of common language, religion, political, cultural and social traditions, were divided. The islands south of Singapore, including Java and Sumatra, went to the Dutch. Peninsular Malaysia and north-west Borneo remained under the British.

The Settlements took a long time turning a profit. In the absence of land revenues and conventional trade taxes, Straits income was limited to excise on rights to sell opium, arak, toddy and other commodities for the locals' 'vices and pleasures'. The budget was not balanced until 1863 when stamp-duties were imposed after the British government took over from the EIC and made the Straits Settlements a crown colony.

Sir Thomas S. Raffles—a symbol of the British presence in South-East Asia.

The EIC's lax administration had attracted a large population—274,000 by 1860, of which 125,000 lived in Penang, 81,000 in Singapore and 68,000 in Melaka. Besides a sizeable Indian minority, the majority were Chinese. Their secret societies regulated coolie labour, settled community disputes and blocked assimilation into the British judicial system. They also fought among themselves over trade in prostitutes and coolies. The British numbered just a few hundred in Penang and Singapore and scarcely a handful in Melaka. From 1826, British law was technically in force (except for Muslim custom), but in practice Asian community affairs were run by merchant leaders serving as unofficial *kapitans*.

Apart from the few Malays in the settlements' rural communities of Province Wellesley and the Melaka hinterland, most still lived inland along the middle reaches of the rivers, away from the coastal marshlands dominated by the *orang laut* pirates. Unity among them and the east coast communities trading with the Thais, Indochinese and Chinese came from their shared rice economy, language, Islamic culture and the political and social customs inherited from the Melaka sultanate. Their economy remained modest and self-sufficient, lacking the modernization and growth that could have created a powerful State.

After the painful experience of the American Revolution, the EIC conducting business from the islands of Penang and Singapore epitomized the British policy of insulating colonies from local politics. Province Wellesley merely acted as a mainland buffer for Penang, and Melaka similarly turned its back on affairs in

23

the hinterland. When Kedah and Perak sought British help against Thailand, the British sided with the Thais to quell revolts—anything for a quiet life. But in the 1870s, under the Colonial Office, the handsome profits gained from exporting Malayan tin through Singapore forced the British to take a more active role in Malay affairs.

The lucrative tin mines of Kuala Lumpur in the State of Selangor, of Sungai Ujong in Negeri Sembilan and of Larut and Taiping in Perak were run for the Malay rulers by Chinese managers providing coolie labour. Chinese secret societies waged constant gang wars for the control of the mines, bringing production to a halt at a time when world demand for tin was at a peak. In 1874, Governor Andrew Clarke persuaded the Malay rulers of Perak and Selangor to accept British Residents as advisors in their State affairs. In return, Britain offered British protection and mediation in the conflicts—the thin end of a thereafter ever-expanding colonial wedge.

It began badly. Within a year, the high-handed Resident in Perak, James Birch, was assassinated after brazen efforts to impose direct British government. Subsequent British advisers served on a consultative State council alongside the Malay ruler, chiefs and Chinese *kapitans*. Birch's successor in Perak, Hugh Low (1877–89), proved more diplomatic. He spoke Malay, was familiar with local custom and religion, and respected chiefs and peasants alike. The reforms he got the ruler to accept—organizing revenue collection, dismantling slavery, regulating land—were precisely the changes which Birch had sought but for which his arrogant approach got him murdered.

The peninsula's unity was enhanced by the expanding network of railways and roads. Governor Frederick Weld (1880–87) extended the residency system to Negeri

Kuala Lumpur's railway station, completed in 1911, pays homage to the local culture whilst proclaiming Britain's industrial might.

Medical Improvements
Efficient colonialism recognizes that disease is unproductive. The British campaign against malaria on the Malay plantations—fighting mosquitoes with swamp-drainage and chemical spray—served as a model throughout the tropics. Progress was also made against beriberi (a form of paralytic dropsy), while Chinese community leaders sought British help in attacking opium addiction. Government supervision of production and sales served at least to control quality, if not to cut down consumption. Opium was also the Singapore government's largest source of income into the 1920s.

Sembilan and the more recalcitrant Pahang, where the ruthless Sultan Wan Ahmad was forced to open the Kuantan tin mines to British prospectors. For Johor, astute, tough-minded Sultan Abu Bakar avoided protectorate status by going to London to negotiate a straight alliance, getting a Consul rather than a Resident. In exchange, he agreed not to extend Johor's rule to neighbouring States. He even helped the British crush a Pahang revolt by chiefs in the interior who resented the Resident's abolition of slavery and forced labour. This cooperative spirit guaranteed him access to Singapore as a market for Johor's agricultural products.

A Federation of Malay States—Selangor, Perak, Negeri Sembilan and Pahang—was proclaimed in 1896 to coordinate an economic and administrative organization. Frank Swettenham became first Resident-General of the Federation, with Kuala Lumpur as the capital.

The White Rajahs of Borneo
In the 19th century, Borneo remained relatively undeveloped. Fierce Balanini pirates, fervent Muslims, disputed the coast of north-eastern Borneo (modern Sabah) with the sultanate of Brunei. Sarawak's coast and jungle interior were controlled by the Iban—Sea Dayak pirates and Land Dayak slash-and-burn farmers. (The Dayaks practised head-hunting, a ritual that was believed to bring vital spiritual energy to their communities.) The region was unproductive and without great resources, except for the Sarawak river valley where the Chinese mined for gold and antimony (a high-quality tin-like mineral used in alloys). Brunei chiefs traded the metals through Americans in Singapore.

Shipwrecked British sailors rescued by Regent Hasim of Brunei in 1839 provided a pretext for Singapore to look into Borneo's potential. The governor sent James Brooke (1803–68) to thank the regent and promote trade links.

Brooke was born in Bengal, the son of an EIC official. He had been an audacious cavalry officer in the Anglo-Burmese wars and now exploited the situation for his own account. In exchange for helping the regent end a revolt of uppity Malay chiefs, Brooke was made Rajah of Sarawak in 1841, with his capital in Kuching (founded by the Malays just 11 years earlier).

He ran a veritable fiefdom, keeping out Singapore entrepreneurs and seeking from London the protectorate status granted to the Malay Federation. In close contact with 'his people', he tried to halt the Dayaks' piracy and head-hunting while defending their more 'morally acceptable' customs.

On a trip to London, Brooke was toasted and knighted for his 'civilizing' influence in Sarawak. But the Colonial Office found his rajah's title a bit too much and refused to make Sarawak a protectorate. Jealous business rivals trumped up accusations of atrocities against the Dayaks while quelling their piracy.

Back in Sarawak, he faced a revolt of Chinese gold-miners. More virtuous than Francis Light had been in Penang, Brooke had tried to block rather than promote their opium trade. The rebels came downriver from their camp at Bau and attacked his Kuching home, murdering his officials. Brooke escaped by swimming across the river. His counterattack with Dayak warriors drove the Chinese out of Bau across the Sarawak border. Thereafter, Chinese settlement was discouraged and did not achieve the commercial dominance it enjoyed on the peninsula.

In 1863, Brooke retired to Britain a broken man, stricken with small-

pox and embittered by Singapore's hostility and the lack of Colonial Office support. He handed Sarawak over to his nephew Charles. More reserved and remote but a better administrator and financier than his uncle, Charles Brooke imposed on his men his own austere, efficient style of life. He brought Dayak leaders on to his ruling council but favoured the time-honoured colonial practice of divide-and-rule by pitting one tribe against another to keep the peace. He led head-hunting expeditions of downriver Dayaks against belligerent tribes in the interior.

North-east Borneo (Sabah) was 'rented' from the Sultan of Brunei by British businessman Alfred Dent. Dent was operating a royal charter for the British North Borneo Company—a charter similar to that of the EIC. But lack of clear leadership stunted the growth of the modest tobacco trade from Sandakan on the east coast, as London-based directors, the Colonial Office and Singapore all had a say.

In 1888, Sarawak, Brunei and what is now Sabah were at last grouped together as a British protectorate: North Borneo. But it didn't gain the status of a crown colony, and hence its economy never benefited from colonial development funds.

Into the Twentieth Century
The British extended their control by prying away Terengganu, Kelantan and Kedah from the Thai sphere of

influence (in exchange for financing the Bangkok-Alor Setar railway). The Malay rulers were not consulted, the Sultan of Kedah complaining that his State had been 'bought and sold like a buffalo'. The States reluctantly accepted British advisers but were not incorporated into the Malay Federation. The peninsula received the whole panoply of colonial administration—civil service, public works, judiciary, police force, post office, education and land regulation—with teams of British administrators teachers, engineers, doctors and to go with it.

The tin industry, dominated by the Chinese with labour-intensive methods in the 19th century, passed increasingly into Western hands, who employed the modern technology of gravel pumps and mining dredges. Petroleum had been found in northern Borneo, at Miri and in Brunei, and the Anglo-Dutch Shell company used Singapore as its regional depot for its oil supplies and exports.

But the major breakthrough for the Malay economy was the triumph of rubber. It had made a disastrous start. The first Brazilian rubber seedlings brought from London's Kew Gardens to the botanical garden at Singapore in 1876 died on arrival. Others remained a scientific curiosity, while European planters turned to the more promising Brazilian import, coffee, until the market collapsed in the 1890s. By that time, Singapore's new garden director, Henry Ridley—Rubber Ridley to his friends, Mad Ridley to all doubting Thomases—had de-

Rubber trees were introduced in Malaysia in the 1870s and rubber manufacture gradually developed to reach its peak during World War I. It is still an important factor in the Malaysian economy.

veloped new planting and tapping methods and painstakingly spread his faith in rubber around the peninsula.

World demand increased with the growth of the motor car and electrical industries, and sky-rocketed during World War I. When Mad Henry retired in 1911, rubber cultivation had grown from 140 hectares (345 acres) in 1897 to 250,000 hectares (617,500 acres). By 1920, Malaya was producing 53 per cent of the world's rubber output, which had overtaken tin as its main source of income. Large-scale financial and technological resources gave Europeans an advantage over the Chinese. The bulk of the labour force were Tamil Indians from the sugar and coffee plantations, supplemented by workers brought in from southern India.

The Malay ruling class again took a back seat. Together with effective control of the rubber and tin industries, the British now firmly held the reins of government. The sultans were left in charge of local and religious affairs, content with their prestige, prosperity and security.

The census of 1931 served as an alarm signal for the Malay national consciousness. Bolstered by a new influx of immigrants to meet the rubber and tin booms of the 1920s, non-Malays now outnumbered the indigenous population by 2,230,000 to 1,930,000. The Great Depression of 1929 stepped up ethnic competition in the shrinking job market and nationalism developed to safeguard Malay interests against the Chinese and Indians rather than the British imperial authority.

Though hampered by the peninsula's division into States and the Straits Settlements, relatively conservative Muslim intellectuals and community leaders came together at the Pan-Malayan Malay Congress in Kuala Lumpur in 1939. In Singapore the following year, they were joined by representatives from Sarawak and Brunei. A more left-wing movement, fostered by technical and training colleges, gave rise to the Union of Malay Youth. Teachers and journalists urged the revival of the common Malay-Indonesian consciousness, split by the Anglo-Dutch dismemberment of the region in the 19th century. This spirit became a factor in the gathering clouds of war.

The Japanese Occupation (1941–45)

The Pacific War began not at Pearl Harbor but 70 minutes earlier, on Malaya's east coast, near Kota Bharu. It was there, at 15 minutes past midnight local time on 8 December 1941 (when it was still 7 December on the other side of the International Dateline in Hawaii) that Japanese troops landed from assault vessels on Sabak Beach (see p103).

Then under embargo by the Americans, British and Dutch because of its war with China, Japan was desperate for raw materials—not least Malaya's rubber, tin and oil and the port of Singapore through which they passed. A 'Greater East Asia Co-Prosperity Sphere', so Japan seductively called it, would be the ultimate aim of this invasion. And again in Burma, the Philippines and Indonesia, Japan appealed to Malay nationalism to throw off the Western imperialist yoke in a movement of Asian solidarity—an 'Asia for the Asians' spearheaded by Japan's Imperial Army.

Not expecting a land attack, British defences centred on its Singapore naval base, leaving Commonwealth troops on the peninsula ill-prepared. Indian infantrymen inflicted heavy losses from their bunkers on the beaches but finally succumbed to the massive onslaught. The landings were launched from bases ceded to the Japanese by Marshal Pétain's French colonial officials in Indochina and backed

(Above) Victims of the Peninsular War against the Japanese are buried in the Taiping War Cemetery. (Right) Kuala Lumpur's National Monument commemorates the 12-year Emergency struggle against communist guerillas.

up by new high-performance fighter planes. The Australian pilots' clumsy, outdated aircraft were no match.

More Japanese infantry poured in from Thailand to capture key airports in Kedah and Kelantan. To counter the Kota Bharu landings, the British overseas fleet's proudest battleships, the *Prince of Wales* and the *Repulse*,

---

On Your Bikes

The Japanese advance rolled through the peninsula not only in tanks, which the British had insisted could never get through the jungle, but also on bicycles. Allied Intelligence in Japan had already been puzzled when it learned, long before the invasion, that the Imperial Army had placed an order for 6,000 cheap bicycles. Infantrymen turned into 'cavalry' as they wheeled down the ramps of their assault craft and along the country roads towards Singapore. Many more vehicles were commandeered from peasants by soldiers in civilian clothes who infiltrated the towns disguised as bicycling coolies.

---

sailed north. But without air cover, they were spotted off the coast of Kuantan and sunk by Japanese bombers. The Singapore naval base was left empty. Kuala Lumpur fell on 11 January , 1942, and five weeks later, the island of Singapore was captured after heavy street-fighting. Northern Borneo was quickly overrun, but the oilfields of Miri and Brunei were pre-emptively sabotaged by the British and Dutch.

If Japanese treatment of Allied prisoners-of-war in Malaya was notoriously brutal, the attitude towards Asian civilians during the Occupation was more ambivalent. At first, the Japanese curtailed the privileges of the Malay rulers and forced them to pay homage to the Emperor of Japan. But then, to gain their support, the Japanese upheld their prestige, restored pensions and preserved their authority at least in Malay custom and Islamic religion. For them, then, things were no worse than under the British.

The Chinese, especially those identifying with Mao Tse Tung's combat against the Japanese, were at first massacred in their thousands, but later courted as middlemen for Japanese-run business operations. From 1943, Chinese communists led the resistance in the Malayan People's Anti-Japanese Army, aided by the British to prepare an Allied return. The Japanese wooed Malay Indians as recruits for a short-lived 'Indian National Army' to fight the British in India. But rubber-plantation workers were also exploited as slave-labour to build the Thai-Burma railway. In Borneo, Iban tribesmen distinguished themselves by reviving, with British approval, the noble art of head-hunting aimed at unwary Japanese patrols who ventured too far into the jungle.

Insurrection and Independence

The Japanese surrender after the bombing of Hiroshima and Nagasaki made a reconquest of Malaya unnecessary, leaving in place a 7,000-strong resistance army led by Chinese communists. Before disbanding—and stashing away its weapons in the jungle—the army wrought revenge on Malays who had collaborated with the Japanese. This in turn sparked off a brief wave of racial violence between Malays and Chinese, dramatizing the ethnic conflicts that would hamper the post-war quest for national independence. (The Japanese experience had at least made an end to British rule inevitable.)

To match their long-term stake in the country's prosperity, the Chinese and Indians wanted political equality with the Malays. Nationalists in the new United Malays National Organization (UMNO) resented this 'foreign' intrusion imposed by 19th century economic development.

To give the Malays safeguards against economically dominant Chinese and Indians, the British created in 1948 the new Federation of Malaya. Strong central government under a High Commissioner left considerable powers in the hands of the States' Malay rulers. Crown colony status was granted to Northern Borneo and Singapore, the latter excluded from the Federation because its large Chinese majority would have 'upset' the population balance. The Chinese, considering that they had been more loyal to the Allied cause in World War II, felt betrayed. Some turned to the radical solutions of the Chinese-led Malayan Communist Party (MCP).

Four months after the creation of the new Federation, three European rubber planters were murdered in Perak. They were the first victims in a guerrilla war launched from jungle enclaves by communist rebels using the arms caches left there by the disbanded Malayan People's Anti-Japanese Army. The British sent in massive troop reinforcements, but the killings continued, mainly European managers in the tin and rubber industries. The violence reached a climax in 1951, with the assassination of High Commissioner Henry Gurney.

His successor, General Gerald Temple, stepped in to deal with the 'Emergency'. He intensified military action, while cutting the political grass from the communists' feet. Templer stepped up self-government, increased Chinese access to full citizenship and admitted them for the first time to the Malayan Civil Service.

Under Cambridge trained lawyer Tunku Abdul Rahman, brother of the Sultan of Kedah, UMNO's conservative Malays formed an alliance with the English-educated bourgeoisie of the Malayan Chinese Association and Malayan Indian Congress. Amid the turmoil of the Emergency, Chinese and Indian community leaders were eager for compromise. The Alliance won 51 of 52 seats in the 1955 election on a platform promising an equitable multiracial constitution.

Independence or 'freedom' (*Merdeka*) came in 1957 and the Emergency ended three years later. The Alliance's English-educated élite seemed to imagine that multiracial integration would come about through education and employment. With a bicameral government under a constitutional monarchy (see p15), the independent Federation made Malay the compulsory national language and Islam the official religion. Primary school education might be Chinese, Indian or English, but secondary education must be Malay.

Tunku Abdul Rahman, the first prime minister, reversed his party's anti-Chinese policy by offering Singapore a place in the Federation. With the defeat of Singapore's moderate Progressive party by left-wing radicals, Tunku Abdul Rahman feared the creation of an independent communist State on his doorstep. As a counterweight to the Singapore Chinese, he would bring in the North Borneo States of Sabah and Sarawak, granting them special privileges for their indigenous populations and funds for the development of their backward economies. (Unable to agree on a formula for incorporating its oil wealth in the Federation, Brunei chose to remain separate.)

To embrace the enlarged territory, the Federation took on the new name of Malaysia in September 1963. Singapore soon clashed with Kuala Lumpur over Malay privileges which Singapore, with its multiracial policies, sought to dismantle. Its effort to reorganize political parties on a social and economic rather than ethnic basis misread the temper of the Malay masses. Communal riots broke out in 1964 and Tunku Abdul Rahman was forced by his party's right wing to expel Singapore from the Federation. Singapore wept all the way to the bank. Under Lee Kuan Yew and the successors he supervised with a paternal hand, its port and service industries have made it, after Japan, the wealthiest country in Asia.

But under 'the businessmen's Prime Minister', Datuk Seri Dr Mahathir bin Mohamad, Malaysia has also achieved remarkable prosperity. After a boom during the Korean War in the 1950s, rubber has suffered competition from synthetic products, though demand remains steady. Tin has continued as an important source of income, but has plastics competition to contend with. This has been supplemented by the spread of lucrative palm oil plantations, the discovery of rich new reserves of petroleum and natural gas off the north coast of Borneo and the east coast of the peninsula, and development of manufacturing and tourism industries. Timber, which in the 1970s and 80s brought valuable revenue to Malaysia as a whole and Sabah and Sarawak in particular, has been cut back to preserve and replenish the dwindling rainforests.

While ethnic conflicts continue, they rarely flare into the kind of violence such rivalries foster elsewhere in the world. Apart from some strict but not fanatical fundamentalists on the east coast, Islam in Malaysia is a quite easy-going religion. In troubled times, Malaysia plumps wherever possible for the good life.

RELIGION

To the outsider, public life in Malaysia may sometimes seem like one religious holiday after another. Muslim, Hindu, Buddhist and other Chinese creeds are each celebrated with fervour, solemnity or merriment as the occasion demands, and Christianity, in a minor mode, also finds its place. The most conspicuous highlights are the prolonged Chinese New Year festivities, then Islam's Ramadan month of fasting followed by a joyous Hari Raya, later the Indian Deepavali festival of lights, and lastly Christmas (Muslim, Chinese and Indian lunar calendars change the dates from year to year. While Islam is resolutely affirmed as Malaysia's official religion, most other major faiths are observed here with a tolerance that contrasts sharply with ethnic conflicts at the political or economic level. It is not extraordinary to see both mosque, pagoda, temple and church built on the same street.

The annual festival of Thaipusam attracts thousands of devotees. Religious fervour often leads to acts of mutilation.

Islam

Observed by 53 per cent of the population, mostly Malays, but also some Indians, Pakistanis and Chinese, Islam was first introduced by Arab and Indian Gujarati traders. Its earliest trace is an inscribed stone of the 14th century found in Terengganu. Using the Arabic alphabet, the Malay text records religious and social laws of the era. From 1400, the religion was spread through the peninsula by the Melaka sultanate. Today, there is no national head of Islam, but each sultan or ruler serves as leader of the faith in his state (guaranteeing that no non-Muslim can become a state ruler).

The world of Islam makes no distinction between a secular life and a religious one. *Muslim* is Arabic for 'one who submits'. The Koran is the revelation of God to Mohammed by the Angel Gabriel. In addition to injunctions against wine, pork, gambling, usury, fraud, slander and figurative representation, it regulates all aspects of everyday life—the way to greet each other, the way to wash, the way to eat.

The Five Pillars of Faith assuring the believer a place in paradise are: *Shahada*: affirmation that 'There is no god but God; and Mohammed is His Prophet.'
Salat: prayers five times a day—

dawn, midday, late afternoon, sunset, after dark—on a prayer-mat facing Mecca (notice arrows on hotel-room ceilings and other public places indicating direction).

Zakat: alms to the poor, gifts to the mosque.

Sawm: during the month of Ramadan, fasting and strict abstinence in all matters from sunrise to sunset.

Hajj: pilgrimage to Mecca at least once in a lifetime.

Almost all Malaysian Muslims are orthodox Sunnites. They approve the historic order of succession of Mohammed's first four heirs and accept the traditions as laid down in the *Sunna*, a 9th century collection of Mohammed's moral sayings and anecdotes.

A minority of Shiites, mostly of Pakistani origin adhering to the Iranian variation of Islam, accords the divine line of succession only to Mohammed's cousin Ali and his sons Hasan and Husein. Shiites, from the Arabic *shiah* ('sectarians'), reject the oral tradition of the *Sunna* and differ from the Sunnites in law and ceremony. The Shiites' fanatic sects like the Fatimites and Assassins had no place here, but their great Sufi mystics preaching the individual soul's union with God found many affinities with Malay animism.

The grand mosque in Shah Alam, west of Kuala Lumpur.

Buddhism

Besides the Chinese, Malaysia also has small communities of Thai, Burmese and Sri Lankan Buddhists. Together, they make up 17 per cent of the population.

Early Chinese and Indian travellers brough Buddhism to the peninsula, most notable I Tsing, a 9th century Chinese pilgrim from Srivijaya (see pp16–17). But it did not take hold until Chinese traders came to Melaka in the 15th century, gaining an even more solid footing with the influx in the modern industrial era.

With their 3,500 temples, societies and community organizations, the Chinese practise the *Mahayana* ('Greater Vehicle') form of Buddhism which evolved in the 1st century BC. Its emphasis on social life has great appeal for the layman. Symbolized by the *Bodhisattva* ('Enlightenment Being'), the incarnation of compassion, buddhism preaches universal salvation and welfare for all. With the aid of Buddha, anyone can gain access to the divine emancipation of *nirvana*.

The more rigorous form of Buddhism, known as *Hinayana* ('Lesser Vehicle'), is practised by the Thais in the northern states of Kelantan, Kedha and Perlis, the Burmese in and around Penang, and Sri Lankans south of Penang and Kelantan with headquarters in Kuala Lumpur.

As for the *Theravada* ('Doctrine of the Elders'), it is considered the

(Left) Joss sticks are lit and prayers made to Guan Yin, the Goddess of Mercy. (Right) Hindu boy.

original version of Buddhism with canon direct from the mouth of Buddha in the 6th century BC. It preaches individual redemption, salvation by one's own efforts, and observation of the moral, ascetic rules of life. The way to *nirvana* is by the Eightfold Path: right views, resolve, speech, conduct, livelihood, effort, recollection and meditation.

Hinduism

As the country's earliest organized religion, pre-Islamic Hinduism of the Brahman priestly caste reinforced the authority of the Indian ruling class. Relics of that era remain in temple ruins, with a *lingam* (sacred phallic-shaped stone) in Kedah (see p94). Its rituals survive in Malay weddings and other ceremonies, and the *Ramayana* epic of Indian divine heroes is used in traditional shadow-theatre.

Unlike Buddhism or Islam, Hinduism has no founding sage or prophet or fixed canon and can claim to be truly eternal and universal. The vast pantheon of Hindu gods has something for everyone: mysticism and metaphysics for the scholars, colourful ceremony for ordinary people, austerity and sensuality, gentle tranquillity and violent frenzy.

Modern Hinduism has been shaped by 19th century immigration from the Indian subcontinent, each regional influx bringing with it its own forms of worship. The largest contingent and most powerful influence were Tamil labourers from southern India and Sri Lanka (Ceylon). Theirs is the populist cult to Shiva, the dancing destroyer-god wearing a garland of skulls with snakes around his neck and arms. Temples have been built on almost every plantation worked by Indian labourers. Universal deities are worshipped in the towns, the best known temple being Kuala

Lumpur's Sri Mahamariamman Temple. Also in the capital, the smaller northern Indian community worships at the Lakshmi Narayanan Temple.

The unifying concept of all Hindu tendencies is *karma*. Literally 'work' or 'deed', it implies the sum total of a person's acts in a previous existence, determining his or her station in this life. For the present, it holds out the promise of a better reincarnation. Hindus say we cannot escape our *karma*, but that with good judgement and foresight we can use it to our advantage.

Confucianism

For most Malaysian Chinese, this moral and religious system coexists with Buddhism to lay down an ethical code of conduct defining man's place in society, from mightiest ruler to the humblest peasant and worker. The sage Confucius (6th century BC) preached self-control, good deeds, personal morality and proper observation of ritual.

Classical Confucianism regulates relations between father and son, husband and wife, elder and younger brother, prince and subject, and between friends. In modern times, it has been the basis of the largely conservative attitudes of Chinese community leaders in Malaysia.

Christianity

Malaysia has about 1,000,000 Christians, most of them living in Sabah and Sarawak, where they make up a third of the population. They are largely the result of Catholic and Methodist missionary work since the 19th century, but many of the Catholics are of Eurasian origin, dating back to the Portuguese colonization of Melaka. They keep a relatively low profile, but Christmas is widely celebrated and Easter is a public holiday in Sarawak and Sabah.

Chinese New Year celebrations.

THE JUNGLE

To go to Malaysia without setting foot in the jungle would be to miss an essential beauty of the country. You must put aside your normal requirements of comfort and ease. The jungle is not air-conditioned. It is always humid and, except for the early hours of the morning and at higher altitudes, always hot. The paths are not always clearly marked.

As for the forest's dreaded beasties, very few are really dangerous. Most of Malaysia's spiders, for instance, are totally innocuous, although many are of impressive size. Tigers have dwindled, sadly, to a tiny, precious few and leopards make a point of keeping out of your way. Even the nasty little leech to which you may donate some blood in the wetter parts of the forest is nice enough to inject a small dose of local anaesthetic, as well as a per-

fectly harmless anti-coagulant. But beware of snakes—of the country's 111 species, only 17 have venom lethal to humans. The general rule is to avoid them: wear hoods and colourful patterns as protection.

But the rewards far outweigh the discomforts. A walk in the jungle can be a rare sensual pleasure. Sounds flood in from all sides: the buzz and whine of crickets, the chatter of squirrels, the poop-poop-poop of hornbills, the cries of gibbon apes.

The Malaysian jungle is home to the orang-utan and countless species of plants.

Your eyes must adapt from the deep gloom of the densest forest to a sudden burst of brilliant sun in a clearing, playing endless variations on the textures and myriad shades of green in the leaves, ferns, mosses, palm fronds and creeping liana.

Five Kinds of Jungle

Old jungle hands like to talk of 'tropical rainforest' while botanical purists go for 'tropical evergreen moist forest'. They distinguish between *primary* or virgin forest and *secondary* forest, where new vegetation has grown in areas of selective logging for commercial timber or on abandoned plantations that were 'clear-felled'. Variations in soil, slope and altitude give rise to five different types of forest:

Malaysia's wildlife is both prolific and luxuriant. Here, a hibiscus hybrid provides a splash of colour.

Mangrove Forest Mangrove trees and shrubs grow on coastal marshland in the brackish zone between the sea and freshwater. They perform a natural land-reclamation with the dense undergrowth of their aerial prop roots. The fruit and leaves feed crabs whose waste products in turn feed fish, prawns and molluscs. Thus, good mangrove tracts make Sandakan in Sabah a major centre of the seafood industry. The mangrove's distinctive companion is the low trunkless nipa palm, whose curtain of fronds has traditionally provided roofing material for coastal huts. The large flower buds are tapped for sugar but, due to the awkward terrain, not on a commercial scale.

Freshwater Swamp Forest Abundant fruit trees in the fertile alluvium of river plains attract a prolific wildlife—waterfowl, elephants, banteng oxen, macaques and, in Sarawak and Sabah, the dynamic proboscis monkeys and our cousins, the orang-utans. Peat swamp, found in the southern half of the peninsula and Sarawak on Borneo, is less fertile but rich in hardwood timber. Where swamp gives way to dry land, you will see the fascinating, monstrous strangler-figs.

Dipterocarp Forest The botanical term refers to the two-winged fruit (similar to the 'key' of the common sycamore) borne by a large number of the forest's tallest trees. This dryland rainforest is what you will see most frequently from just above sea level up to an altitude of 900m (3,000ft). Its wealth of trees is remarkable: 835 different species have been counted in 50 hectares (125 acres) of the Pasoh Forest Reserve in Negeri Sembilan, compared with under 100 over the same surface area in the richest European or North American forest.

The forest's tallest and perhaps most handsome tree is the *tualang*, found both in the northern half of the peninsula and in Sabah and Sarawak. The *tualang* rises to 75m (245ft). Bees like to build their combs in its upper branches because the smooth-barked trunk makes it hard for bears—and humans—to climb up and steal the honey. The Borneo ironwood or *belian* produces the world's densest, hardest timber after the South African ironwood. But

Sabah boasts the fastest-growing tree in the world: an acacia-like *Albizzia falcataria*, which was 'clocked' from germinated seed to 10.74m (over 35ft) in just 13 months. Although many trees are known to be several hundred years old, it is impossible to estimate a Malaysian tree's age accurately because lack of seasonal changes leaves none of the annual growth rings observed in temperate climates.

Making It Easier

You can visit the jungle on your own, but to enjoy the mysteries of the jungle's plants and wildlife to the full, we recommend that you enlist the help of a local guide who knows the terrain and its lore. If you go on a trek without a guide, make sure that somebody outside the jungle knows roughly where you are heading. People do get lost.

Good canvas walking shoes are essential. For longer visits, take a light bag with changes of T-shirts, underwear and socks, a good pocket-torch (flashlight) with spare batteries, a pair of binoculars and some insect-repellent. If you do fall victim to leeches, relax, it's no real disaster. A pinch of salt rubbed on their bodies or placing the lit end of a cigarette near them will cause them to stop 'eating' and to drop off. After discarding the little pest, salt from your own sweat should stop the bleeding—some recommend tobacco or toothpaste. Then add a cleansing dab of alcohol.

45

If you were expecting to see a wild variety of brightly coloured flowers or exotic fruit on your visit, you might be disappointed. At any given time of year, only 2 per cent of the dipterocarp forest's plants and trees bear fruit or flowers, mostly from July to September. Most fruits are not all that tasty or soft, but look out for mango, breadfruit and the wild rambutan, a sort of bright red hairy lychee. Durian are large spiky balls with a creamy flesh that smell awful to a European nose and delicious to the Malaysians.

Heath Forest Poor soil on the flat terrain leading to foothills or on sandy mountain-ridges produces only low, stunted trees with thick leaves. The heath forest is remarkable for its profound silence compared with the jungle's incessant din elsewhere. Only an occasional rhinoceros or barking deer passes through, and few insects other than ants. The ants are welcome residents in the *Hypnophytum* plant which grows out of the trunk of various trees. The plant's distinctively bulbous 'chambers' provide a home for the ants, which earn their keep by chasing away noxious caterpillars and nourishing the plant with their waste products.

Montane Forests Here, at 1,200m (4,000ft) and above in large mountain ranges, or as low as 600m (2,000ft) on small isolated mountains, the large trees and liana creepers give way to myrtle, laurel and oak trees. Wild raspberries appear along with magnolias, rhododendrons, orchids and other epiphytes (plants that grow on other plants but are not parasites, since they procure their own food supply). Boulders are covered with a fascinating array of mosses. One of the most intriguing specimen of montane flora (also found in the heath forest) is the

---

Life and Sudden Death of a Rafflesia

During his tour of duty as lieutenant-governor in Sumatra (see p22), Stamford Raffles and botanist Joseph Arnold discovered in 1818 a huge bright orange-red flower that proved to be the largest in the world. Its full name is Rafflesia arnoldii, *though Arnold rarely gets a mention. Looking more like a cabbage than a flower, with petals spreading out to 90cm (3ft) in diameter, this leafless parasite needs a wild grape vine known as* Tetrastigma *for its essential nutrients. It is found only in Malaysia and Sumatra, at an altitude of 500 to 700m (1,600 to 2,300ft). The bud takes from 9 to 18 months to blossom, and that happens suddenly, usually after rain, bursting into full flower at around midnight. Within a couple of days, decay sets in and the awesome giant gives off a smell of bad meat to attract flies to carry its pollen. You are more likely to see it at Sabah's Mount Kinabalu National Park, where a special effort is made to preserve and propagate this rare plant.*

pitcher plant. The pitcher is not a flower or fruit but a leaf-like structure. Hanging invitingly from the top of the plant, it fills with rainwater, waits for insects to crawl in and gobbles them up for their much appreciated nitrogen and phosphorus.

Animal Life

Unlike the wildlife of the African plain, the animals of the Malaysian jungle are not very conspicuous. While we might like to see them, they would just as soon not see us and it is much easier for them to hide. The exceptions, of course, are the inquisitive, noisy monkeys and apes chattering and rattling around in the trees. The vegetation of the rainforest does not favour the antelope family and other big grass-eaters. Thus the deer, elephants, wild cattle, tapirs, pigs and rhinoceroses are in too small numbers to attract large predator cats. Tigers and leopards remain a rarity.

Like the human race, large mammals are inhibited by the hot humid climate. Unable to lose their sweat in the saturated forest, they seek out the cool of muddy pools, rivers and deep shade. When it comes to comfort, small is best. The elephants, rhinos, tigers and bears of Malaysia are therefore the smallest of their kind. Again, like their human neighbours: forest-dwelling aboriginal *orang asli* are much smaller than other Malaysians.

Here are a few animals that you will see with luck and perseverance:

Elephant About 1,000 elephants are scattered across the peninsula, notably in the Taman Negara National Park, and perhaps twice that number in eastern Sabah. A few of them have been domesticated for plantation work. They are daintier beasts than their African cousins. Most noticeably, they do not have the Africans' huge ears, and the tusks, not present in all males, are much shorter. Shoulder height is 2.5m (8ft)—compared with 4m (13ft) for the African elephant—and they weigh in at a mere 5,200kg (11,440lb)—a good 800kg (1,760lb) less than the African. Females and their young roam in herds of 10 to 12, usually in single file, occasionally joining up with other herds to form a group of 30 to 50. Except for mating time, the males are strictly loners. The females' pregnancy lasts 18 to 22 months. Life expectancy is 70 to 80 years. Elephants like to eat grass, palm tips and the stems of wild banana and ginger plants, at a rate of some 150kg (330lb) a day for a full-grown beast.

Rhinoceros Scarcely a hundred remain of the Sumatran Rhino on the peninsula and in Sabah, and the best place to see it is at the Sepilok sanctuary, where controlled breeding hopes to combat the ravages caused by poaching. The horns are coveted for the 'aphrodisiac' qualities which the Chinese attribute to them when ground to powder. In fact, the horns consist of two not very fierce pointed mounds of compacted hair. (The horns' chemical properties are the same as claws, hooves or toe-nails, so that people seeking a cheap and ecologically less harmful aphrodisiac might just as well chew their finger-nails.) The rhino, a truly prehistoric monster practically unchanged for 30,000,000 years, eats a tough diet of twigs and thick leaves to keep up its weight of 1,000kg (2,200lb). It is nat-urally a loner but will occasionally share a mud-wallow with one or two others. To see it in its wild or semi-wild state, follow its distinctive three-toed footprints to a cool pool in the Sungai Dusun Wildlife Reserve north-west of Kuala Lumpur, or in the Tabin reserve in eastern Sabah.

Tapir This animal is remarkable for two things: 1. its short overlapping snout that resembles the sawn-off trunk of an elephant; 2. its unique body-colouring—black up front, white in the middle and back, with black rear legs. It is found only on the peninsula. Your best chance to see it is at the Ampang reserve near Kuala Lumpur or at Taman Negara. A creature of habit, the tapir follows the same beaten track for years and favours a fast-moving river.

Deer Most common are the tiny mouse-deer. These timid nocturnal beasts sport a brown coat speckled with white. They rarely measure more than 55cm (22in) from head to stumpy tail and shoulder height is 33cm (13in). They have no antlers but medicine men sell fakes that are in fact long teeth. The largest Malaysian deer is the brown antlered sambar. Another shy creature, you might spot it at the edge of the forest or on river banks. About 2.7m (9ft) from head to tail, it stands at 1.5m (5ft) at shoulder height. The barking deer, so-called because it bays like a dog when threatened by predators, wears a shiny reddish-brown coat. Its antlers seem to grow out of a second pair of ears that are really supports of skin-covered bone,.and serve in quite violent mating-duels. Hunters lure females by blowing through a leaf to imitate the high-pitched sound of their young.

Tiger The few Malaysian tigers left roaming the peninsula are the smallest of the breed, weighing only 200kg (440lb), 100kg (220lb) less than the Indian or Chinese tiger. To track down its prey (usually deer or wild pigs), this solitary predator may stake out a territory of up to 1,000sq km (400sq miles), pa-trolling it regularly and marking it with droppings.

Leopard The 'classical' spotted yel-low or black coat of the leopard may be seen not only in the jungle but also around plantations and farms. The smaller clouded leopard hunts up in the trees, enjoying a varied diet of monkeys, baby orang-utans, birds and squirrels. The leopard-cat is not a lot bigger than our domestic cat and may nip in and out of villages.

Bats, Birds and Butterflies

A major Malaysian adventure is cave-exploration, so be ready for an encounter with the only flying mammals. Literally hundreds of millions of bats inhabit the caves of Malaysia, so you can only expect to meet a few of them. They are completely harmless and none of them are blood-sucking. For instance, flying foxes– wing-span 1.5m (5ft)—look fierce up close but are strictly vegetarian. Bulldog bats just *smell* horrible. If you really hate bats, be at the cave-mouth at twilight when they emerge en masse for supper ... and hawks wait around to pounce on any slowcoaches.

Birdwatchers in the dipterocarp forest tot up 60 species a day. A good location is around strangler figs when the fruit is ripening. The fig tree attracts yellow-crowned barbets (a puffbird member of the woodpecker family) and helmeted hornbills, notable for the mad cackle that punctuates their poop-poop-poop. In secluded valleys, you can spot eagles, hawks, owls and the lovely blue and red garnet-pitta, a ground-dwelling gourmet that likes lizards and snails.

The colours you might miss in exotic flora are supplied in delightful variety by the butterflies. The national butterfly is the 'Rajah Brooke Birdwing' identified by the bright green markings on its black wings spanning up to 18cm (7in). It was discovered by the naturalist Alfred Russel Wallace and dedicated to James Brooke, first White Rajah of Sarawak (see pp26–7). Other beauties are the 'Common Tree Nymph', with its dark spotted buff-coloured wings, 'Dark Blue Jungle Glory' and 'Swallowtail Red Helen'. One of the country's most spectacular winged creatures is the huge 'Atlas' moth, in brilliant shades of orange and yellow.

Orang-utans are relatively discreet forest-dwellers, best seen at Sabah's Sepilok wildlife reserve.

nose is an unremarkable little snub, but zoologists say that she appreciates, and is even aroused by the male's proboscis. They frequent mangrove swamps and rivers, swim well and can best be seen on the lower Kinabatangan river in eastern Sabah and the Bako and Samunsan nature reserves in Sarawak. Dayak hunters consider them a gourmet delicacy.

Orang-utan In Malay, *'orang-utan'* means 'forest person'—an appropriate mark of respect for the mammal biologically closest to man. These highly intelligent russet-coloured apes live in the swamp forests of Sabah and Sarawak, and are best seen in eastern Sabah's Sepilok wildlife reserve. They are very individualistic nomads, meeting occasionally to share a fruit supper before going their own way. From the age of four, the orang-utan makes a new nest every night, a nest that consists of a round platform of leaves and twigs woven around a forked branch. The nests are good pointers to their favourite stomping grounds, as they are otherwise much more discreet than gibbons or macaque monkeys. Standing erect—an extremely rare occurence—adult males would be 1.5m (4ft 7in) tall, whilst their arm span is a huge 2.5m (7ft 10in). They weigh around 75kg (165lb). Some visitors to Sepilok confuse them with the similarly coloured red-leaf monkeys—but unlike monkeys, orang-utans have no tails.

Proboscis Monkey Unique to Borneo, it is the male that sports the splendid pendulous nose that gives the species its name. It is also the male who emits a formidable honk through its nose at times of great excitement or alarm. The female's

WHERE TO GO

Setting your priorities in Malaysia before you start out is essential to making the trip both pleasant and satisfying. Improvisation is fun, but if you are not used to the hot and humid climate (a constant but not necessarily hostile factor), a little planning will avoid unnecessary stress.

At the back of the book, the blue pages provide detailed practical information on how to handle your stay in Malaysia. Here we provide some general ideas before describing the places you will be visiting.

Starting in Town

The towns hold a fascinating mirror to Malaysia's special ethnic blend of Malay, Chinese, Indians and Eurasians, living side by side or in their separate neighbourhoods. This takes on a metropolitan dimension in Kuala Lumpur. (In true Malaysian style, we will refer to the capital by

its affectionate abbreviation, 'KL'.) The east coast around the town of Kota Bharu is the best place to see traditional Malay life with its rich Muslim culture, particularly evident in the *kampongs* of the interior. Catch a glimpse of the sultans' grandeur at Kuala Kangsar in Perak. In Melaka, observe the way of life of the *Babas*, the oldest Chinese community, and its more modern manifestation in Penang. But remember when visiting places of worship to dress in an appropriately dignified manner and to slip off your shoes before entering a mosque or a Hindu temple.

The museums are few but well worth a visit for a sense of the country's history, culture and folklore. The major ones are in KL, Melaka, Penang, Kuching and Kota Kinabalu. And the picture of life on the peninsula is best completed with a visit to Singapore's national museum—if you happen to be passing through.

A Quiet Life

Why did Malaysia in ancient times never develop the kind of great monumental art of which neighbours Thailand, Cambodia and Indonesia are so justly proud? The answer is largely to do with geography. Spared the natural calamities like earthquakes and typhoons that plagued their neighbours, the peninsula and northern Borneo developed tranquil clusters of small village communities but no large urban populations. Impenetrable rainforest made communications difficult and the monsoon limited contact along the coasts. Infertile mangrove swamp and mountainous jungle defied the kind of large-scale agriculture that fosters large centralized states with their monumental temples and palaces. Later on, the architecture of the Malay sultanates lacked permanence because the main building medium remained perishable wood.

Heading Out to the Country

But you will soon want to get out to the wonderful green world beyond the city limits. Finding your way around the riches of rainforest, coral reef and marine biology can be bewildering if you plunge in unprepared. Unless you already have some experience of the region, we recommend that you use the services of the many first-class local tour operators. For jungle-tours, they provide experienced English-speaking guides, most of them with a good knowledge of the rainforest. Offices of the Malaysian Tourist Develop-

Transport in Malaysia can be as fast or as slow as you like.

ment Corporation in your home country can provide guidance to the most reputable companies (see p186). Most operators have their headquarters in KL and organize tours nationwide. They may sub-contract to smaller but equally reliable companies in outlying regions.

Malaysia has done a fine job of giving visitors access to its natural treasures without 'taming' them too much. At the heart of the peninsula, the huge Taman Negara gives you the most comprehensive view of the country's animals and plants in their wild state. A more 'compact' approach is possible on the islands, notably with excursions into the wilderness of Tioman or Langkawi. If you are attracted by the egg-laying habits of turtles, head for Rantau Abang in July and August.

On the island of Borneo, the great natural attractions are Sarawak's caves at Niah and Mulu, river cruises with a visit to tribal longhouses, Sabah's national parks of Mount Kinabalu and the offshore islands, and the Sepilok wildlife sanctuary.

And Then the Beach

For many, the beach may be the be-all and end-all of a vacation. Malaysia has much, much more to offer, but it would be silly to avoid the beach altogether. Wash off the jungle sweat with a dip in the sea. On the west coast, the best beaches are at the island resorts of Penang and Langkawi. But you will find more unspoiled stretches of fine sand on the east coast, from Pantai Chinta Berahi, north of Kota Bharu, down to Beserah, north of Kuantan. Further south are the resorts of Tioman Island and Desaru. In East Malaysia, Kuching and Kota Kinabalu both have fine hotel resorts.

Speaking the Language

Though the official tongue is Malay, or *Bahasa Malaysia*, English is still the common language of communication between Malays, Chinese and Indians. After an initial nationalist resistance to using English to accompany Malay road signs, a new effort is being made to accommodate foreign drivers. But you may still like to use a few words of Malay as a courteous gesture to your hosts.

You will find a more comprehensive list of useful phrases in the blue pages at the back, but here are some words to be getting on with:

apa khabar?	how are you?
baik	fine
maaf	excuse me
terima kasih	thank you
selamat jalan	good-bye (to person leaving)
selamat tinggal	good-bye (to person staying)
selamat pagi	good morning
selamat malam	good night
nama saya ...	my name is ...

And one expression you will see everywhere:

selamat datang!	Welcome!

53

THE CENTRE

The heart of the peninsula surrounds Kuala Lumpur with a concentration of economic riches, cool highland resorts far from the torrid plain and the bewitching rainforest of the nation's beginnings. The western coastal states flank the capital with tin mines, oil palm and rubber plantations, shipping out at Port Klang. Ipoh is Perak state's most flourishing tin town, Taiping a bustling creation of Chinese diligence, Kuala Kangsar the leisurely, royal state capital from which the sultan surveys his assets.

In Pahang to the east, Genting Highlands, Fraser's Hill and above all Cameron Highlands are the closest thing the British could find to their cooler native climate. Strawberries, cabbages and, thank the Lord, tea plantations still flourish there, as do golf courses and a casino. The vast Taman Negara, which translates as 'National Park', is one of the best preserved primary rainforests in the world, at once accessible to the public and lovingly protective of its plants and wildlife.

KUALA LUMPUR

Look a little harder among the capital's gleaming skyscrapers and you will spot here and there a quaint neo-Gothic mansion or a Palladian villa. They are the 19th and early 20th century residences of the tin magnates whose wealth turned this patch of reclaimed swampland from a rough, tough mining camp into a thriving metropolis, one of the most prosperous in Asia. And the thick growths of ferns palm trees, creeping liana and *lallangs* in the 'gardens' or abandoned construction sites remind you that the jungle is a

The capital's towering high-rises all but dwarf Kuala Lumpur's mosque.

constant companion inside the city limits. In 1974, Kuala Lumpur gained its autonomy from the state of Selangor, thus becoming a separate Federal Territory. But above all, the capital is a vivid compendium of Malaysia's past and present.

Street and shop signs are printed in Roman, Arabic and Chinese characters. As in other Malaysian towns, the population is predominantly Chinese. The Chinese community is prominent in the modern business world, while the traditional old Chinatown is a bustling quarter of low-slung shophouses. It stands cheek by jowl with a Little India of pungent spice shops and ornate Hindu temples. Malays make their presence felt in the upper echelons of government, civil service and tourist offices.

The Historic Centre

Start where Kuala Lumpur started, at the confluence of the Klang and Gombak rivers near the junction of

55

Jalan Tun Perak and Jalan Raja Laut. A pleasant grassy triangle marks the point where supplies were loaded to be sent upriver to the tin mines at Ampang. Here, too, the tin arrived for shipment west to Port Klang. Today, against a sweeping backdrop

The distinctive Sultan Abdul Samad Building bears more than a passing resemblance to Big Ben.

of skyscrapers, the Chinese tin-miners have given way to Muslim worshippers padding across the cool white marble floors of the **Masjid Jame mosque**. It was designed in 1907 by A.C. Norman and A.B. Hubbock in what must be described as British Imperial Indian Moghul style: three pointed domes over the prayer hall, two minarets and white balustrades above an arcade of cusped arches—the whole predominantly gleaming white, with pink terracotta brick. Non-Muslims are welcome inside, except at times of prayer. (You must also remember to remove your shoes and dress with appropriate decorum.)

Behind the mosque across the river is the city's most distinctive old edifice, the **Sultan Abdul Samad Building**. The handsome crypto-Moorish Federal Secretariat, now the Supreme Court, was built in 1894 and capped with three fine copper onion domes. One tops a 41m (135ft) high clock tower that gives the British game away, its clock clearly Big Ben inspired.

Running along the building's western façade is the wide green **Padang** or field that once echoed to the genteel knock of bat on ball. For it was here that members of the mock-Tudor **Selangor Club** (1884) on the other side of the field took time off from the affairs of the Empire to play cricket. Unlike India, Pakistan and other former colonies, independent Malaysia has not taken to the British national summer pastime. The Padang now hosts National Day state parades and more frequently—not so cere-monious but just as colourful—after-dark rendezvous for transvestites. A carnival-like spirit has long prevailed here: when the river overflowed its banks and flooded the green, members of the Selangor Club could—and did—swim across to their offices in the administrative HQ that is now the Sultan Abdul Samad building. On Sundays, they showed a little contrition for their excesses by making an appearance at the rather undistinguished Anglican **church of St Mary's** (1894) on the north side of the Padang.

Among the many impressive new skyscrapers, one of the most striking complexes is the **Dayabumi** (1985), south-east of the Padang. Housing governmental offices and the headquarters of Petronas, the national oil company, the soaring 34-storey white tower successfully integrates traditional Islamic architectural themes—pointed arches, delicate open tracery—with its otherwise modern design. On Saturdays, trips are organized to the top of the tower, starting out from the fountain between the Dayabumi and the adjoining **General Post Office** (Pejabat Besar Pos), in similar Islamic modern.

At **Infokraf**, by the Dayabumi, the Malaysian Handicraft Development Corporation has a permanent exhibition of national craftwork, with many exhibits for sale.

> *Getting Around*
> *The expressways and major highways criss-crossing the city can make orientation difficult. If you intend renting a car, keep it for excursions out of town such as the Batu Caves and the hill stations. For those in a hurry, an air-conditioned minibus tour will take in the major sights, but you will not get a feel for the neighbourhoods. Otherwise, we recommend using a taxi—where the meter is not in use, ascertain the rate before starting off—and then walking around. Downtown is perfectly safe and people are very friendly, always ready to show you directions. Take a little pocket notebook to note addresses, not least your own hotel telephone number in case you get lost.*

Across the river going east is the old **Central Market** (Pasar Seni), set in an attractive art deco building (1936) in pastel blue and pink with a bold bright skylit roof over a buff-tiled floor. Clothes and Malaysian arts and crafts have displaced the fish, meat and vegetables that used to be on sale here, but the fine old marble counters are still in place.

The ultimate symbol of the British Empire in KL is the astounding **Railway Station**, south on Jalan Sultan Hishamuddin. A major instrument of Britain's industrial might in the 19th century, the railway was the natural means of asserting economic and political power throughout the peninsula. Just as rail stations in London, Birmingham or

57

Manchester were veritable cathedrals erected to the glory of the Industrial Revolution, so KL's railway station (completed in 1911) resembles nothing so much as a gleaming white mosque-cum-sultan's-palace. Above the arcades of tall Moorish cusped arches are domed minarets from which one might imagine a *muezzin* announcing the arrival of the next train. Though the façade pays a rather fanciful homage to the local culture, the British imposed true-blue Victorian specifications on the building—the roof structure being delayed until it could meet the need of holding up under one metre of snow. KL railway station comes complete with a more subdued grey-stone Railway Administration Building. Next door is a **National Gallery** (Balai Senilukis) of Malaysian and foreign art, housed in the old colonial Majestic Hotel.

Chinatown

Epitomizing the dominant role that the Chinese continue to play in Malaysia's urban life, Chinatown is without a doubt the most colourful and liveliest neighbourhood in KL. It is situated south of the Central Market, beyond Jalan Cheng Lock. Shophouses and street stalls cluster around its main axis, **Jalan Petaling**. The merchandise is both traditional and up to date, but the atmosphere has not changed much since 1900.

In the early morning before the invasion of traffic, market stalls sell fish, seafood, poultry, fruit and vegetables. Grocers offer pickled eggs, shark fins and dried fish. The quarter teems with dry-goods stores, pet shops, haberdashers, goldsmiths and ironmongers. Apothecaries sell herbs, roots, seeds, spices and concoctions of ancient cures for modern ills. The future is in the hands of fortune-tellers.

At night, Jalan Petaling is closed to traffic, giving way to pedlars selling watches (bewildering replicas of designer brands), music and video cassettes, clothing, jewellery and ornaments. The side streets are full of open-air restaurants offering dishes of barbecued pork, duck and seafood, noodles, rice-pots and do-it-yourself 'steamboats'.

The spiritual and social centre of Chinatown is the **Chan See Shu Yuen Temple**, at the corner of Jalan Petaling and Jalan Stadium. Built in 1906, it is an elaborate and gaudy affair, with glazed ceramic dragons and other fiery monsters guarding the gods in an intricate network of pavilions and courtyards. Like many other Chinese temples throughout Malaysia, it serves both as a place of worship and as a meeting hall or clan-house for community associations.

KL's Hindus gather at the **Sri Mahamariamman Temple** on Jalan Bandar, on the west side of Chinatown. It was built in the style of a south Indian *gopuram* (temple gatehouse-tower), covered with a riot of colourful statuary from the Hindu pantheon. First erected in 1873, it was shunted across to its present site to make way for the railway station in 1885. Girls sell jasmine necklaces and other trinkets outside the temple and an old man is there to look after your shoes if you want to go inside.

The National Monuments

West of the railway station, the **Masjid Negara** (National Mosque) is a vast, modern complex covering over 5 hectares (13 acres). On Fridays and other major prayer days, it houses some 8,000 worshippers under the tent-like stone roof of its Grand Hall. Walls of openwork stone tracery support a canopy of 18 folds fanning out in a circle. These symbolize the 13 states of Malaysia and 5 pillars of Islamic faith. The mosque also includes ceremonial rooms, a library, a meeting hall and a mausoleum for national heroes, set around cool pools mirroring the blue stained-glass of the Grand Hall and marble galleries. Soaring above it all is a 73m (239ft) high minaret, with a graceful balcony from which the *muezzin* calls the faithful to prayer.

West of the National Mosque are the spacious **Lake Gardens** (Taman Tasik Perdana). These 70 hectares (170 acres) of parkland were landscaped in 1888 under British Resident Frank Swettenham for the citizens' relaxation. It is a popular place for picnics, jogging and siestas beneath the trees, features an artificial lake for boating and is now also the site of the **National Monument** (Tugu Negara). Set on a hill at the

Marriage Malay Style

Today's marriage dowry may subtly combine ancient decorative tradition with unabashed modern materialism. A close look at a bride's floral arrangement in the National Museum reveals that the roses are intricately folded red $10 notes, the lilies are blue $1 and the leaves green $5 notes. Modern attitudes have also diminished parental negotiations prior to a Malay marriage, but otherwise much old custom persists, if only in symbolic form. It is a typical mixture of Islamic law, ancient Malay tradition and rituals borrowed from the Hindus.

To mark agreement on the dowry and duration of the engagement, a women-only ceremony, berinai kecil, takes place at the bride's home to stain her feet and fingertips with henna. The wedding contract, akad nikah, can then be signed and the hands of both bride and groom stained with henna—berinai besar.

The next day, bride and groom are enthroned side by side, bersanding, to receive the guests into the bride's home. Yellow rice and rose-scented water are scattered to welcome the groom's family and friends, who return the compliment to the happy couple. The guests each receive a coloured boiled egg, symbol of fertility. A traditional Malay sword dance, pencak silat, is performed with jolly comments about its symbolism.

The wedding night is also spent in the bride's home and thereafter the husband takes over.

northern end of the park across a main road, the monument commemorates the 12-year Emergency struggle against communist guerrillas (see p33). The bronze group sculpture stands in an attractive setting of reflecting pools and fountains with a mosque at one end. It was designed by Felix de Weldon and bears a striking similarity to his Iwo Jima Memorial to the Pacific War in Washington, D.C. Triumphant flag-bearers are flanked by armed guards while another soldier helps a wounded comrade. Beneath them sprawl the enemy's dead. Malaysians criticize the monument for its absence of any clearly Asian types among the victorious soldiers. Also on the National Monument grounds is a cenotaph to the British Commonwealth's dead of the two World Wars. West of the Monument, just outside the park, is the 18-storey **Parliament House** which holds the sessions of the Senate and House of Representatives.

The **National Museum** (Muzium Negara) stands on Jalan Damansara south of the Lake Gardens. The building, built in 1968, blends modern with traditional Malay design. Two glass mosaic murals flanking the entrance depict themes of Malaysia's culture and history. There is a small entrance fee to the fully air-conditioned museum.

While opening times are inevitably subject to unannounced changes, it is normally open every day—except for two days of the

---

Bleeding and Burning Faith

The Batu Caves (right) are the focus of the great Thaipusam Festival celebrating Lord Murugan receiving a sacred spear with which to vanquish the sources of evil.

Every January or February thousands of Hindus gather to do penitence for past sins. The most fervent of them punish themselves by having their tongues or cheeks pierced with skewers, hooks pierced into their body. Some also carry a kavadi (a frame bearing peacock feathers and statuettes of deities. Some simply carry jars of milk, rose-water, coconuts or sugar-cane juice. During Thaipusam, as many as 500,000 people will crowd around the Batu Caves.

For infidel tourists, the climb in humid heat up 272 steps to the cave-shrine entrance may be penitence enough. Beneath the caves lie dozens of underground limestone vaults.

Hari Raya festival at the end of Ramadan—from 9.30 a.m. to 6 p.m., closed Friday from 12 to 2 p.m.

Up on the first floor, where temporary exhibits are shown in the central hall, the gallery to the right is devoted to Malaysian history and culture—arts and crafts, weapons, medals and the life and lore of the peninsula's *orang asli* aborigines. The gallery to the left exhibits the country's natural history with showcases and dioramas of mammals, birds, butterflies and insects. The second floor is given over to

fascinating scale models of equipment used in the nation's tin, rubber and forestry industries.

Away from the City Centre

To see the remaining **tin magnates' mansions**, take a taxi ride on Jalan Ampang, leading north-east from the city centre in the direction of the old Ampang tin mines, 10km (6 miles) out of town. A few of these grand 19th- and early 20th-century residences survive tucked away among the skyscrapers, the jungle often invading the gardens. Most drivers will be able to point out the **Bok House**, transformed into the elegant *Coq d'Or* restaurant. Built in American colonial style with neo-classical columns, it was the home of Chua Cheng Bok, a legendary rags-to-riches entrepreneur who gave up the old iron of his bicycle repair shop for a fortune in tin and other businesses.

If you are visiting the modern shopping centres on and around Jalan Bukit Bintang, east of Chinatown, take a look at the nearby **Pudu Prison**, famous for the long mural painting of jungle and *kampong* motifs on the outside wall. It was executed by a prisoner, under armed guard, who finished his sentence before completing it, leaving to become an artist in a Hong Kong advertising agency.

At the other end of Jalan Bukit Bintang is the **Karyaneka Handicraft Centre**, a good place to find representative artwork from all over Malaysia—useful if you cannot get around the whole country.

Since the Central Market closed down its food stalls, the most colourful food market is now out in the garish northern suburb of **Chow Kit**, on Jalan Raja Bot, off Jalan Tunku Abdul Rhaman—at night a red-light district. East of Chow Kit is the Malay quarter of Kampong Bahru, site of the **Sunday Market** (Pasar Malam), which in fact, in keeping with Muslim custom, starts at sunset on Saturday evening. You will find pewter from Selangor, silverware from Kelantan, embroidered silk from Terengganu, hand-painted batiks and earthenware pottery. It is also a good place to sample traditional Malay food—*satay* barbecued chicken and seafood.

DAY TRIPS FROM KL

Batu Caves

Transformed into a Hindu shrine, the Batu Caves are a popular excursion 45 minutes' drive north of town just off the Ipoh road. Set in limestone cliffs hidden in the jungle, they were discovered last century by a group of British explorers, including the American naturalist William Hornaby, while chasing moths. In 1891 Hindu priests appropriated the caves as a sanctuary for the Lord Murugan.

There are in fact dozens of underground limestone vaults attracting botanists and zoologists to their unique flora and fauna, but only three are open to the general public. At the top of a 272-step staircase, you will reach the shrine in the **Cathedral Cave**, taking its name from the architectural columns of its lofty stalactites and stalagmites. At the foot of the hill, a bridge over a pond leads to the **Art Gallery Cave**, displaying garish statues of Hindu deities, and the **Poet's Cave**, where the verses of ancient Tamil poet Thiruvalluvar are painted on stone tablets. These two-line *kural* verses deal variously with morals, wisdom, love and finances. At the foot of the caves are some good Indian vegetarian restaurants.

Templer Park

If you do not have time to visit Taman Negara (see pp74–7) or the jungles of Borneo, Templer Park, 20km (12 miles) north of KL makes an ideal introduction to the Malaysian rainforest. After making his name in jungle warfare against communist guerrillas, Britain's last High Commissioner, General Gerald Templer, conceived the park as a 'vast jungle retreat for the public'. Covering an area of 1,200 hectares (3,000 acres), the rainforest comes complete with waterfalls, rushing streams, lagoons for swimming and caves to explore in the Bukit Takun limestone cliffs. But well marked paths reassure you that this is still a park, and not impenetrable jungle—a fact reinforced by the presence of two golf courses at the base of Bukit Takun.

THE HIGHLANDS

By the time Malaysia came under the British imperial sway, colonial officials had fully developed that grand institution of the hill station where they could cool off from the hot and humid lowlands. These havens of relaxation set among golf courses, gardens and orchards still dot the mountain ranges of the peninsula's interior, but they are now holiday resorts under Malay, Chinese or Indian management. With its cool mists and rolling hills, the landscape was as close as the colonial officers could find to their native Scotland, Wales and England, and so you will often find vegetables, fruit and freshwater fishing more familiar to Europeans than Asians. But the jungle is still there—the highlands were major rebel strongholds during the Emergency—so exploring it is not like a simple walk in the woods. The usual precautions apply about informing others if you are going off by yourselves.

Cameron Highlands

The finest of the cool colonial retreats stands on a splendid plateau of rolling green valleys surrounded by rugged granite peaks, the tallest of which is Mount Brinchang at 2,032m (6,664ft). Although explored and warmly recommended by British surveyor William Cameron in 1885, it was not developed as a hill station until 1925, when it became used principally for market-gardens, tea plantations, and weekend homes for wealthy rubber planters.

It is best reached by train on the main KL–Butterworth line to Tapah Road station and then by taxi up into the hills. Driving yourself on the narrow winding road with frequent back-ups imposed by lorries in a hurry could be a hazardous business. Let the taxi driver worry about that while you admire the magnificent scenery changing from lowland mangrove, bamboo and palms to denser rainforest of lush greenery and, as the heat drops away to a comfortable 24°C (75°F), to montane oaks and laurels familiar to temperate climates.

The first of the Cameron Highlands' three townships is the Ringlet, an unprepossessing place although interesting as a distribution centre for farm produce—tomatoes, spring onions, cabbages, lettuce, even asparagus—that you would not expect to find in the tropics. Just beyond the town is the attractive man-made Sultan Abu Bakar Lake, fed by the waters of the Bertam River.

The main towns are **Tanah Rata** and **Brinchang**, where you will find the best shops, some good Chinese and Indian restaurants and more or less quaint tea rooms serving the local Cameronian brew with cakes, locally grown strawberries and cream. On the outskirts are rolling vistas of the green, green tea plantations.

Among the comfortable hotel resorts, the ivy-covered mock-Tudor **Smokehouse**, set in a charming flower garden on the way to Brinchang, is something of an institution. Even if you are not staying there (relatively expensive), this comic pastiche of an English country inn is worth a visit for a traditional 'cream tea' on the terrace, beer in the bar or a meal in the rather genteel restaurant. Nearby is a fine 18-hole public **golf course**, beautifully kept despite the strange hazard of a narrow concrete-sided canal running across the middle of it.

The cooler climate makes **jungle walks** here a special pleasure, not least of all for the myriad brightly coloured butterflies around the waterfalls. But be especially careful as maps available at the hotels and in Tanah Rata are at best sketchy. The two most clearly marked paths from Tanah Rata, easiest for the whole family, lead within an hour to a refreshing swim at **Parit Falls** or **Robinson Falls**. Others more challenging, for which you should enlist the help of a guide, take you up to **Mount Perdah**, 1,576m (5,169ft), **Mount Jasar**, 1,696m (5,562ft) and **Mount Beremban**, 1,841m (6,038ft). Besides the butterflies, look out for red-bellied squirrels, wild pig and, if you are lucky, an occasional tapir. Even if you do not spot the siamang apes, you cannot escape their crazy whooping. You may also witness the phenomenon of birds banding together in 'gangs' of different species to stir up the insects and eat them.

(Above) A 'little England' in Malaysia: Ye Olde Smokehouse in the Cameron Highlands.

The local **Butterfly Farm** is probably your best chance of seeing the grand 'Rajah Brooke Birdwing' and other rare species. You can also take a guided tour of a **tea plantation**, at the Boh Tea Estate, Sungei Palas, or Blue Valley to see how the tea is gathered and processed.

Fraser's Hill

This charming old-fashioned hill station, 100km (60 miles) north-east of KL, is built across seven hills, its highest point being 1,310m (4,296ft). It was founded by Louis James Fraser, an adventurous scoundrel

65

(Previous page) A refreshing sight: tea plantations in the Cameron Highlands. (Above) A tea plucker.

who dealt in mule hides, tin, opium and gambling. It is much more respectable now. If you are doing the driving, be careful on the narrow road. Over the last 8km (5 miles), traffic is one-way on an hourly alternating basis.

The countryside is wilder, less cultivated than the Cameron Highlands. But the sedate side of colonial life is also more recognizable here in the white and greystone bungalows with roses, rhododendrons, poinsettias, hollyhocks and dahlias in the gardens. There are good tennis courts and a 9-hole public golf course. Once up there, you may like to rent a bicycle.

The wealth of wildlife makes **jungle rambles** particularly enjoyable. Head for a swim at **Jeriau Waterfall**, 4.5km (2 miles) north of town. The orchids and ferns are beautiful, and the soaring fishtail palms, up to 30m (98ft) high, truly impressive. Birdwatchers look out for racket-tailed dongo, hornbills and the migrant Siberian thrush. This is also one of the rare areas where you might catch a glimpse of a tiger.

Genting Highlands

Uncharacteristically modern in atmosphere, this is more of a gambling resort than a hill station. One hour's drive from KL (10 minutes by helicopter for players in a hurry), Genting Highlands offer skyscrapers, a cable car, an artificial lake, a swimming pool, tennis and squash courts up top and golf course down below. But above all it has a **Casino** which lays on the usual Western gaming tables as well as Chinese games such as *Keno* and *Tai Sai*. The Chinese are the most avid customers. Notices proclaim that men must wear ties or long-sleeved batik shirts and that Muslims are not allowed in. (The casino is air-conditioned.)

PERAK

The state of Perak is one of the proudest in the Federation. The sultan's family is the last able to trace its ancestry back to the 16th century sultans of Melaka. The state's name means 'silver' and it is the craft of Perak silversmiths at the sultan's court that is now revived by Kelantan craftsmen on the East Coast. But the shining metal that made the state's modern fortune was tin. Its capital, Ipoh, may be considered the capital of the world's tin industry. It superseded Perak's other rich mining centre, Larut, now renamed Taiping— still a fascinating reminder of the old backbone of the peninsula's economy.

The journey north from KL either by train or car takes you through a captivating landscape of jungle reaching back from the coastal plain to climb the blue hills of the Barisan Titiwangsa range. Amid this wild beauty, enhanced by spectacular outcrops of limestone rock, are the tell-tale scars of the tin mines of the Kinta Valley.

Ipoh

Built on the west side of the Kinta Valley 220km (135 miles) north of KL, the tin-rich capital of Perak was, like KL itself, originally just a landing stage for miners. Use the town as a base for exploring the surrounding country.

Today, Cantonese Chinese run the tin mines and dominate the town.

The magnates have built their handsome mansions in the green and shady suburbs. Ipoh is also a home from home for connoisseurs of Chinese food. Seek out, opposite the police station in the city centre, the open-air restaurants serving the local speciality—heavenly steamed chicken, bean sprouts and noodles.

Memories of the British are present in the **clock tower** commemorating British Resident James Birch, assassinated in 1875 (see p24), **St Michael's School** and the **railway station**, whose style is amply described by its local nickname, the 'Taj Mahal'. But the most poignant monument to the old imperial dream is the **Royal Ipoh Club**. It has all the old trappings of an Englishman's club—even if the Chinese and Indian members do not keep up the tradition of cricket on the adjoining green field. (The club is private, but people with an English accent have been allowed in for a peep 'just for old time's sake'.)

For an insight into the local tin mining, visit the excellent **Geology Museum** out on Jalan Harimau. In addition to exhibits of Perak's rich variety of minerals, ores and fossils are models of tin-mining equipment, including the monumental gravel pumping machinery.

Set in vast caves in limestone outcrops north and south of town are two imposing Buddhist temples: to the south, **Sam Poh Tong**, built in the 1890s, with a rather gaudy new façade added in 1950 and a staircase

of 246 steps leading to the upper shrine; to the north, **Perak Tong** (1926), with its lotus pond, giant seated Buddha 13m (42ft) tall and a mere 385 steps up to a superb view of the Kinta Valley.

(Above) Kualar Kangsar's elegant wooden palace. (Right) The rather gaudy Sam Poh Tong Buddhist temple, in Ipoh.

Kuala Kangsar

The home of the sultans, built on a loop in the Perak River, is a half-hour drive away from Ipoh on the new highway. But if you have the time, it is worth driving along the longer old route to take in the hilly countryside and its many dramatic limestone cliffs pushing up through the jungle. The town has two royal palaces, the brash modern stone residence, **Istana Iskandariah**, and the more elegant traditional timbered **Istana Kenangan**, now used as a Royal Museum. But the most striking building, up on a grass mound, is the **Ubudiah Mosque**, with its massive onion-dome of glowing copper set in a nest of white minarets. Its building in World War I was delayed by a couple of elephants running amok across the marble floor.

Kuala Kangsar has long been famous for its **Malay College**, a prestigious and highly exclusive school for the Malay aristocracy since 1904 but now open to the best (Malay) scholars of all classes. The town also served as a nursery for the peninsula's first successfully grown rubber trees—two of them still standing, near the downtown agricultural offices and up on Government Hill near the old Residency (now a girls' school).

Taiping

Another 30 minutes' drive from Kuala Kangsar, this old mining town was once better known as Larut. Its present-day name, meaning 'Great Peace', was proposed by Britain as its diplomatic contribution to the end of the bloody gang wars in the 1870s.

Happily boasting the peninsula's heaviest rainfalls, Taiping has been able to landscape a magnificent park, **Lake Gardens**, from an abandoned tin mine. The park has a 9-hole golf course, a small zoo and a handsome old **Government Rest House** (now a hotel) combining Neo-Classical Doric columns with a slightly curving Minangkabau roof—ideal for shedding the heavy rains. Also inside the park but less elegant is a prison, used first by the Japanese and then for guerrilla warriors captured during the Emergency.

Built in 1886, the **Perak Museum**, pioneer of the peninsula's museums, houses an interesting display of ornaments, costumes, musical instruments, weapons and farm implements.

Beyond Lake Gardens, the **Taiping War Cemetery** bears impressive witness to the peninsula's early role in the Pacific War against the Japanese. The tombs of men of the Royal Australian Air Force, Indian Army Corps of Clerks, Ambulance Sepoy of the Indian Army Medical Corps and Royal Air Force reveal that many of them died on the very first day of active duty: 8 December 1941.

Once a tea estate, cool, cloud-enshrouded **Maxwell Hill** (Bukit Larut), 1,020m (3,345ft) high, is now a relaxing hill station. Near the jeep terminal, pretty bungalows offer rooms for rent, with balconies overlooking the valley. Before and after the regular afternoon rain showers, take a misty jungle walk—the only sports facility here is a badminton court. Other than a three-hour climb, the one way up is by government-operated four-wheel-drive jeeps every 60 minutes during daylight hours. As an ironic revenge for the torture of Allied prisoners-of-war building roads and railways through the jungles of South-East Asia, Japanese prisoners had to build the steep road up Maxwell Hill.

Kuala Kangsar's Ubadiah mosque, built during World War I, is a splendid jewel of architecture.

TAMAN NEGARA

This grandiose national park provides an ideal setting for exploring vast expanses of rainforest, fast-flowing rivers and mountains of the peninsula's Main Range. It covers an area of 4,343sq km (1,676sq miles), spreading across three states: Pahang, Terengganu and Kelantan.

Backpackers may want to go it alone, but others are advised to plan their visit through a tour operator in KL. Armed with an entry permit, visitors make first for the park headquarters, 300km (187 miles) northeast of the national capital by road via Jerantut and 60km (37 miles) by motor-powered longboat from Kuala Tembeling. (Buy your film, batteries, mineral water, insect-repellent, etc., at Jerantut: everything is more expensive inside the park.)

Fishing Trips
You can rent your angling equipment at the park headquarters and take off by boat to the Tahan river (via the Lata Berkoh rapids) or the more distant Kenyam or Sepia rivers, where you will find 300 varieties of freshwater fish. Most challenging for fishermen used to trout or salmon are the feisty kelah (Indian mahseer). The best times of year are February and March or June, July and August. Self-catering lodges for overnight accommodation are available at Kuala Kenyam and near Lata Berkoh for the Tahan river.

The **boat ride** on the Tembeling River is likely to be one of the highlights of your visit. Along the way, you will see aboriginal Negrito fishermen—the only human residents allowed to stay here by the park authorities—setting or checking their nets. Keep a look out, too, for water buffaloes taking a cool soak, river-lizards slipping in and out of the water and looking as large as crocodiles (the latter do not come this far upstream), and even an occasional otter. Among the birds, you will see the flash of a kingfisher or hornbill. Make sure to wear a hat and to bring along plenty of mineral water. The journey usually takes three hours, even longer when short stretches of the river dry up, forcing passengers to walk along the riverbank while the boatmen push the launch through the shallows.

The headquarters at **Kuala Tahan** have a good range of accommodation—chalets, a hostel and a rest house—plus washing facilities, restaurants and a grocery store—payment is strictly in Malaysian currency. (For your trekking requirements, see p45.) The park headquarters organize evening slideshows as a general introduction to the features of the surrounding rainforest.

Jungle Trails
There are marked trails leading from the park HQ into the jungle. Guides use them for organized walking and boat tours, but you can, of course, go

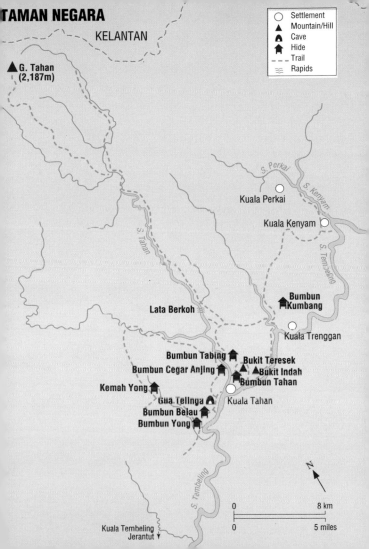

off in your own group. There are both day trips and overnight tours to observation-hides, from where you can watch for wildlife visiting nearby salt-licks and water-holes. Overnight stays are organized at several observation-hides in the region, namely at **Kumbang**, **Yong**, **Tabing**, **Belau** and **Cegar Anjing**. HQ will provide sheets if you do not have a sleeping bag. You should be in the hide by the afternoon and out again the next day at around 9.30 a.m.

From park HQ, day trips leaving in the early morning include:
1. A walk to Bukit Indah, followed by a boat ride through the rapids to **Kuala Trenggan**, returning to HQ on foot;
2. A walk to the **Tabing Hide**, followed by a boat ride to the **Lata Berkoh rapids**, then another trek back to HQ;
3. A boat ride on the Tembeling River to the **Gua Telinga Bat Cave**, which you enter on hands and knees until you can stand. You then find yourself in a great vault inhabited by hundreds of fruit- and insect-eating bats not at all interested in attacking humans. Only the squeamish will object to the giant toads and harmless little white cave racer snakes.

The most adventurous trek for experienced climbers is a full nine-day walk up and down the peninsula's highest peak, **Mount Tahan**, 2,187m (7,173ft) high. A jungle guide accompanies the group.

Flora and Fauna

The dipterocarp rainforest here includes the *tualang* tree. At 50m (164ft), it is the tallest tree in South-East Asia. Among the jungle fruit are mango, durian, rambutan and wild banana. At over 1,500m (5,000ft), you will see montane oaks and conifers.

With patience and luck by day or rotating shift watches by night, you may see wild pigs, sambars and barking deers, gibbons, pig-tailed macaques and leaf monkeys, tree shrews and red flying squirrels. Visitors to the Kumbang Hide have seen rare tiger and leopard.

During the fruit season, bird-watchers have spotted up to 70 species just around the park headquarters. Among them: lesser fish eagle, crested serpent eagle, osprey, peacock pheasant and garnet pitta. From September to March you can also see migrant Arctic warblers, Japanese paradise flycatchers and Siberian blue robins.

Even if you do not spot much of the wildlife we mention—and we promise you will see something—the sheer experience of the jungle at night, with its incredible noises, the flitting of mysterious fireflies and the sense of invisible but omnipresent life and movement around you make it all worthwhile.

The fast and furious Sekayu rapids, in Terengganu.

THE WEST COAST

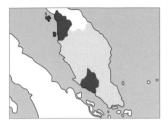

The West Coast has always been Malaysia's window on the world. Along with resourceful Chinese entrepreneurs, Portuguese, Dutch and British colonizers were attracted by the ideal location and port facilities of Melaka and Penang. More recently, tourists have headed not only for these fascinating centres of Asian history but also for the beach resorts of Batu Ferringhi on Penang Island and of Langkawi Island further north.

SOUTH FROM KL TO MELAKA

From the national capital, the route down to the coast at Melaka passes through Negeri Sembilan, literally the 'nine states' federated as one in the 18th century. It is the principal

home of the Minangkabau people, or 'buffalo horn', who migrated from Sumatra in the 17th century (see p21).

Seremban

The state capital created by the 19th century tin boom is surrounded by hills 65km (40 miles) south-east of KL. Its architecture is a pleasant mix of colonial and traditional styles, with Victorian government

The mouth of the Melaka River may have lost some of its bustle of lore, but it remains an important feature of the city.

office buildings on the outskirts, low-slung Chinese shophouses in the city centre, and a generous sprinkling everywhere of Minangkabau buffalo-horn roofs. Notable examples are the **State Legislative Building**, a nest of nine roofs, one for each founding state, and the **Arts and Handicrafts Centre**. In the grounds of the Centre is the splendid **Ampang Tinggi Palace**, a Malay prince's residence brought here and reconstructed in its original form, all wood, no nails. Exhibits of royal costumes and ceremonial weapons are on display inside.

Sri Menanti

For what is probably the best original example of Minangkabau architecture, take a side trip to the old royal capital, 37km (23 miles) east of Seremban on the Kuala Pilah road. The ruler's palace, **Istana Lama**,

has a beautiful wooden shingle buffalo-horn roof and intricate carving on the doors and surrounding pillars.

MELAKA

Malaysia's very first city was, in its glorious 15th-century heyday, the outstanding port in South-East Asia. The capital of the ancient sultanate—fount of Malaysia's modern traditions and religion—still offers the proudest and most colourful testimony to the country's historic past.

Melaka's Chinatown is also the best place in Malaysia to hunt down attractive antiques and bric-a-brac and the atmosphere there is much more relaxed than in KL or Penang's Georgetown.

The Historic Centre

The main buildings of historical or cultural significance are all within easy walking distance of the old centre, Dutch Square, down by the Melaka river. This is also a good place to pick up a trishaw ride around the outlying sights. Save your car for excursions out of town.

The square is situated just off **Melaka Bridge**. Spanning the river, the bridge was once the town's main strategic link between port and city and was the site of major battles against European invaders. The **port** west of the bridge has lost the bustle of its great days but barges and sailing *prau* (boats) still come in from Sumatra and further afield to

trade, with little more than an outboard motor to distinguish them from their ancestors.

The landmark of **Dutch Square** is the **Clock Tower** (Jam Besar), built in 1886 by a Chinese merchant, Tan Beng Swee. In the middle of the square is the **Queen Victoria Jubilee Fountain**, flanked by a mouse-deer recalling the legendary little beast that inspired Prince Parameswara to make Melaka his capital (see p18).

Christ Church was the peninsula's first Protestant church. It was erected by the Dutch in 1753 and built of pink brick imported from the Netherlands, which were then given a coating of laterite. Each of the great long rafters of its interior is hewn from one tree. Equally impressive are the original massive wooden pews.

But the most prominent building overlooking the square is the Dutch **Stadthuys** (Town Hall) built in 1660. Behind its red-brick façade is a structure of masonry hauled from the Portuguese citadel. It has been refurbished to serve as a **Historical Museum** tracing the town's colonial and Malay past.

At the top of the hill, above the square where the Portuguese built their citadel, stands the roofless ruin of their Church of Our Lady of the Annunciation (1521), taking its present name, **St Paul's Church**, from the Dutch. In front of the church tower is a **statue of St Francis Xavier**, its right arm broken

Christ Church, Melaka's Protestant church, goes back to the days of Dutch colonisation.

off during a storm. The Spanish Jesuit missionary visited Melaka four times in 1545 and 1546 and his body was brought here after his death, in 1552, on Shangchuan Island off the coast of Canton. In the church, a stone slab marks his tomb, empty since his remains were taken to Goa, India. Granite tombstones from the Dutch era stand against the walls. A Dutch and British **cemetery** can be found further down the hill.

At the bottom of the hill is the venerable **Porta da Santiago**. This handsome stone gateway was preserved by the intervention of Sir Stamford Raffles, passing through Melaka when his philistine British colonial colleagues were systematically destroying the rest of the Portuguese **A Famosa** fortress. The date 1670 and coat of arms were added to the gateway by the Dutch East India Company.

Set in its own grounds on the other side of Jalan Kota is the **Proclamation of Independence Memorial** (Tugu Pengistiharan Kemerdekaan). With its crypto-Moorish onion domes, it occupies what was once more prosaically known as the Malacca Club or Town House (1912), a watering hole for British colonials. It was on the club's playing field (*Padang*) that future

Prime Minister Tunku Abdul Rahman announced in 1956 the success of his London negotiations for the country's independence. The Memorial building offers films and documents tracing the campaign for independence.

The **Malay Sultanate Palace** (Istana Kesultanan Melayu) stands as a cultural museum amid elegant gardens north of the Porta da Santiago. Reconstructed from ancient prints, it is an approximate but note-worthy replica of Mansur Shah's grandiose hilltop residence which is believed to have burned down in 1460. In homage to the modern Federation, building materials have been brought in from all over the peninsula and East Malaysia. For example, Sarawak's *belian* hard-wood has been used for the roof rather than the tiles of the original. The museum exhibits the splendours of the sultans' regalia, including an impressive **royal bedchamber**. Islamic culture is honoured with some fine wood carvings and an ancient **stone sundial** used for observing the five daily times for prayer.

Chinatown

Nestling in the curve of the river across the Melaka Bridge is the quietly self-confident community of the Babas, the Chinese who inter-married with Malays in the old Straits Settlements—Melaka, Penang and Singapore. In port warehouses, little shophouses and sturdy man-sions, you will find the furniture and finery of their 19th-century and early 20th-century heyday.

The families of rubber magnates and traders took over the houses of the Dutch on **Jalan Hang Jebat** (formerly Jonker Street) and **Jalan Tun Tan Cheng Lock**— 'Millionaires Row'. This is an an-tique hunter's paradise, filled with new and old Oriental treasures— porcelain, statues, jewellery, silver-ware and heavy 19th century fur-niture, the latter 'Victorian' with a decorative Chinese touch. Amongst the antique dealers are basket weavers, blacksmiths, goldsmiths, coffin makers, grocers and apothe-caries, tucked in among some of the handsomest old mansions in all Malaysia.

One of the mansions, at 50 Jalan Tun Tan Cheng Lock, is the **Baba Nyonya Heritage Museum**. Built in 1896 by rubber planter Chan Cheng Siew, this house offers a vivid in-troduction to the life and culture of

Baba Nyonya

The Baba Nyonya community of Melaka (baba, male, nyonya, female) demonstrates the Chinese genius for adapting to local circumstances without losing the essentials of their own culture. Their subtle blend of Chinese and Malay traditions began back in the 15th century when the entourage of Princess Hang Li Poh, daughter of the Emperor of China betrothed to Mansur Shah of Melaka, intermarried with the local gentry. Their numbers were boosted in subsequent centuries by the influx of merchants and entrepreneurs, largely from Fukien in southern China.

The Chinese talent for business made a cheerful union with the Malay taste for pleasure, culminating in the joyously ostentatious affluence of the 19th and early 20th centuries. The Babas made their money from spices, rubber, timber and tin and got their pleasure from gambling, a chew of betelnut or an occasional pipe of opium. Their nyonyas happily spent the family fortune on opulently furnished houses and in preparing an elaborate trousseau for their daughters—bejewelled wedding shoes, gowns and headdresses, glass bead embroidery for bedding-covers and pillowcases.

Silver purses, belts and bracelets combine Chinese and Islamic motifs. The porcelain is decorated with brightly coloured exotic bird and flower motifs, imported from China. But in tribute to the town's 19th-century governors, it incorporates very British soup tureens, eggcups and soap dishes, and stands on a heavy Victorian sideboard. Baba Nyonya cuisine is a similarly triumphant synthesis of southern Chinese delicacies and the spice and pungency of Tamil-influenced Malay ingredients—garlic, red-hot shrimp paste and rich coconut milk.

the Straits Chinese, as the Babas are also known. In a style best described as Chinese Palladian, with its Neo-Classical columns and heavy hardwood doors, the residence bears witness to the great prosperity of Baba entrepreneurs. A member of the Chan family is usually on hand to give you a gracious guided tour of the interior and show you the finer points of the embroidered silks, filigree silver ornaments, gleaming blackwood furniture inlaid with ivory or mother-of-pearl, and monumental gilded teak staircase leading to the bedrooms on the upper floor. Particularly fine is the porcelain —polychrome for everyday use and blue and white for ceremonial occasions. Notice, too, massive lattice wooden screens through which unmarried daughters were allowed to peep at their parents' guests in the drawing room.

Clustered together along Jalan Tokong and Jalan Tukang Emas are Chinese and Hindu temples and a Muslim mosque, coexisting in an ethnic harmony rare in today's troubled world but typical of

Melaka's easy-going atmosphere. The **Cheng Hoon Teng Temple**, originally built in 1645 though transformed many times since, is the oldest Chinese temple in Malaysia. It is flamboyantly decorated with multicoloured birds and flowers of glass and porcelain. The bronze statue of Kwan Yin, the Goddess of Mercy, was brought back from India in the 19th century. The **Kampung Kling Mosque** (1748) is built in the three-tiered Sumatran style with a pagoda-like minaret. The **Sri Poyyatha Vinayagar Moorthi Hindu Temple** (1781) is also one of the oldest in the country. It is the scene of a spectacular full moon festival in February or March, when penitents follow a statue of Lord Vinayagar carried on a chariot to another temple on the outskirts of Melaka.

Outside the City Centre

Rather than drive around the sights away from the old city centre, you may prefer to relax and let the trishaw-driver find the way—and give you the bonus of his wry comments. Start perhaps with an evening ride along the open-air restaurants on Jalan Taman, better known as **Glutton's Corner**. Until the recent land reclamation for new housing developments, these Malay, Chinese and Tamil Indian eating places bordered on the sea front, but the cuisine (the most notable dish being the spicy *mee hoon* noodles) has not changed.

Bukit China

Inland, the hillside provides a Chinese cemetery for over 12,000 graves, mostly horseshoe-shaped tombs. At the top of the hill you will see foundations of the 16th century Portuguese Franciscan monastery and get a splendid **view** over the town to the Melaka Straits. The gaudy red, gold and white **Sam Po Kong temple** stands at the foot of Bukit China, honouring Cheng Ho, the eunuch admiral who in 1409 opened up Melaka to Chinese trade. Nearby is the **Sultan's Well** (*Perigi Raja*) dug in the 15th century for Princess Hang Li Po, whom the Emperor of China had given as a bride to Mansur Shah. Its pure waters were subsequently protected by Dutch fortifications.

The Portuguese Settlement

A short drive some 3km (2 miles) south of the town centre along Jalan Parameswara takes you to the heart of the little Eurasian community, descendants of the Portuguese colonists. Around Jalan d'Albuquerque and **Portuguese Square** (Dataran Portugis), the houses look no different from those in the rest of Melaka, but you may hear snatches of *Cristao*, a 16th century Portuguese dialect, and mothers calling out to 'Afonso', 'Luis' or 'Filomena'. The restaurants on and off the square serve good seafood, though over the centuries the Portuguese cuisine has taken on a spicy Asian flavour. The community worships at the simple, unassuming **St Peter's Catholic Church**, where Easter is an especially big event attracting many Indians, Chinese and Malay non-Catholics to the great candlelit procession.

The Coast Roads

Swimmers should beware of the pollution at the beaches but it is worth taking a ride north along the Jalan Tengkera coast road to visit some of the picturesque fishing villages. On the way, take a look at the fine three-tiered Sumatra-style **Kling Tengkera Mosque**. It is the burial place of Sultan Husain of Johor who negotiated with Raffles the British rights to Singapore. You will find good crab and shrimp at the fishing village of **Pantai Kundor**. Further north, **Tanjung Bidara**, 35km (20 miles) from Melaka, has a hotel

resort and some pleasant tree-shade on the beach for picnics.

Some 8km (5 miles) south of Melaka, you can take a boat at Umbai out to **Pulau Besar island**. Pulau Besar has good white sandy beaches and offers some pleasant walks in the jungle. A resort has recently been opened on Pulau Besar.

PENANG

This most fascinating of Malaysia's many islands is linked to the peninsula by a new toll bridge, one of the country's proudest engineering achievements. You can reach Penang by road or rail from KL to the mainland town of Butterworth, and from there take the ferry across to Georgetown. Or you can fly directly from KL to the Bayan Lepas

---

Sobering Up

The Malays of Melaka must have been quite bemused by the successive waves of European conquerors. When the Sultan of Melaka ran things, the great port was renowned for the opulence of its court life. With his coffers filled by a rake-off from the profits of energetic Indian Gujerati merchants, the sultan's favourite seat was in the lap of luxury. There, he watched slave girls dancing at succulent banquets, where his guests ate from dishes of gold on tables bedecked with the most costly embroidered silks. The Portuguese soldiers, beset with dysentery and malaria, had little energy left for the good life. But they did find time to marry the local girls, who knew all the best cures, and founded the little Portuguese colony that survives in Melaka today. The Dutch merchants were a dour lot who were prepared to make political and military alliances with Malay rulers but not to fraternize with the local populace. They left no Little Amsterdam when they departed. Moving north to Penang, the British did little more than dismantle all the Portuguese fortifications except for one gateway saved by Sir Stamford Raffles, who was passing through. Today, the opulence has gone, but the Malays and Chinese are a lot more fun.

85

Airport at the southern end of the island.

Although it was soon supplanted in its broader roles as a major Indian Ocean trading port and British naval base by Singapore and Trincomalee (Sri Lanka), Penang has continued to play an important part in Malaysian life. The Chinese traders who moved up the coast from Melaka have created a thriving community in Georgetown, where the British left some impressive colonial buildings. More importantly perhaps, Penang cuisine is as esteemed in Malaysia—for its *asam laksa* noodles, *char koay teow* seafood and curries—as Lyon's cuisine in France, Bologna's in Italy or New Orleans's in the States. And, in addition to its glorious beaches, the island also boasts some superb forests and nature reserves.

Georgetown

Under the British, Penang was named Prince of Wales Island and the capital took its name not from King George III but from his son, the future George IV. Today, it is Malaysia's third largest city (after KL and Ipoh) and the focus of the country's electronic industry. The skyline of old colonial government buildings and Chinese temples and shophouses is updated by gleaming new skyscrapers such as the 65-storey **Komtar** civic centre and shopping complex.

Downtown, arcaded walkways protecting you from sun and rain make tours on foot a pleasure. For trips further afield, take a trishaw with its zip-up plastic cover in case of a shower *en route*.

The Old Centre

Even if you arrive by road over Penang Bridge (Asia's longest and a symbol of the island's self-assertive ambitions), begin your tour of the town over at **Weld Quay**. This gives you the historic first view enjoyed by Rudyard Kipling or Somerset Maugham. To the south are the wooden jetties of **Clan Piers**, a hamlet of houses on stilts, linked by wooden walkways over the water and inhabited by 2,000 Chinese fishing folk. Each pier is named after the clan resident in the cluster of houses around it. At the docks, net mending, and the loading and unloading of supplies go on all day.

North of Ferry Pier past the bus station is the landmark of **Penang Clock Tower** (Jam Besar), at the corner of Lebuh Light and Jalan Fort. (As common in Penang as *Jalan* for 'road', *Lebuh* is Malay for 'street'.) The tower is just over 18m (60ft) high, one foot for each year of Queen Victoria's reign when it was erected for her Diamond Jubilee.

Opposite is **Fort Cornwallis** (named after Charles Cornwallis, Governor General of India). Now the

Hop on a trishaw for the best views of the city.

site of a park and playing fields, the fortifications were originally made of wood and rebuilt in stone in 1810, but they had no strategic military importance. The cannons on the ramparts were never fired in defence of the harbour and are put to much better use today as slides for the children's playground. The oldest cannon is the **Seri Rambai**, which turned up here at the end of a checkered career, after being given by the Dutch to the Sultan of Johor in 1606. If you see flowers in its barrel, this

Light in the Jungle

On the north-east corner of the waterfront, Kedah Point marks the spot where the Penang settlement's founder Francis Light (see p22) is said to have hit upon a neat method of getting the surrounding jungle cleared to make way for the town. He loaded a cannon with Spanish silver dollars, fired them into the forest, and invited local labourers to hack their way through the undergrowth to get at their wages.

is no act of some latter-day peace movement but an offering from a childless woman hoping for fertility.

Around the **Padang** green and **Esplanade** stand the dazzling white Neo-Classical government buildings. The Britons worshipped in **St George's Church** (1818) on Lebuh Farquhar. Wander through the picturesque cemetery where frangipani roots wind around the tombs, some resembling miniature Greek temples. Among them is the simpler **grave of Francis Light** who died in 1794 only six years after starting his Penang adventure, a victim of malaria like so many of the young colonial officials buried here.

Francis Light's statue stands at the entrance to the **Penang Museum** at the corner of Lebuh Light and Lebuh Farquhar. In fact, as no other portrait of him was available, the sculpture is in the likeness of his son William (who founded the city of Adelaide in Australia). The museum is housed in the old Penang Free School for the families of the colonial service. Besides documents and artifacts of Malay and local colonial history, the museum has a rich collection devoted to Baba culture (see p83). One incongruous exhibit left behind by the Royal Air Force, and for a long time unidentified, is a bronze bust of German Kaiser Wilhelm II. In the upper-floor Art Gallery are works of 20th century Malaysian art.

One of the great monuments from Georgetown's colonial days is the **Eastern & Oriental Hotel** on Lebuh Farquhar. Even if you are not staying in one of the E & O's grand old rooms—to join the ghosts of Kipling and Maugham—do at least take a drink in the venerable 1885 Bar commemorating the year of the hotel's foundation. The E & O is actually the fusion of two separate hotels: the Eastern, facing the Esplanade, and the Oriental, facing the sea. It was the brainchild of Martin and Tigran Sharkie, Armenian brothers who also created the great Raffles Hotel in Singapore. Its elegant ballroom, bar and restaurant made the E & O the social centre of Georgetown. On a starlit night, the long seafront promenade bordering its gardens still offers one of the most romantic walks in Asia.

Chinatown

Starting opposite the E & O, **Jalan Penang** is Georgetown's main street heading into the business district and forming the western 'boundary' of the main Chinese quarter. The famous **Rope Walk flea market** runs between **Lebuh Campbell** and **Lebuh Chulia**. Here you can wade through literally mountains of old clothes, jewellery, utensils, clocks, dolls, ornaments, old coins and all the bric-a-brac of an oriental bazaar. You will find good leather and canvas gear for your jungle treks on Campbell and Chulia streets themselves.

Wander around the neighbourhood's back streets to admire the beautifully kept residential houses, many with elegantly carved teak window screens and doorways and handsome gold and black lacquered name plates.

More flamboyant are the **clan houses**, bulwarks of community solidarity. They combine temples for ancestral worship with meeting halls to settle local problems—housing, jobs, medical care, help for orphans and discreetly handled intra-community crime. The most prominent is **Khoo Kongsi**, reached via a narrow cobblestoned lane to Cannon Square at the angle of Lebuh Pitt and Lebuh Acheh. The vast, ornate ancestral temple **Leong San Tong** stands opposite a smaller hall used for open-air Chinese opera and theatre. To gain entrance to the temple, get a visitor's pass from the clan office building (off to the right as you face the temple). The temple roof and entrance are a riot of colour, huge flower urns, scarlet tiles, blue dragons and dancing sages, with warrior-giants guarding the doors. From the entrance canopy hang great gilded wooden lanterns among friezes and decorative panels. The Khoo clan's patron saint, Tua Sai Yeuh, a general of the 3rd century BC, has his picture in the central hall of three interior places of worship. To the left is the God of Prosperity and to the right is the hall of *sinchoo* (soul-tablets): gold plaques honouring clan dignitaries and simpler wooden panels for more humble clan-members.

Another example of Chinese conspicuous consumption is the splendid **Cheong Fatt Tze mansion** on Lebuh Leith. This extravaganza was erected in the 1880s by a businessman from Kwangtung. For his seven wives and eight sons he built 24 rooms around cobblestone courtyards. You will see a grand wrought-iron spiral staircase, delicate Art Nouveau stained-glass windows, massive gilded teak lattice screens, embroidered silk wall-hangings and collections of porcelain alternatively gaudy and elegant.

The **Kuan Yin Teng temple**, on Jalan Masjid Kapitan Kling (formerly Lebuh Pitt), is Georgetown's most popular public temple, dedicated to the Goddess of Mercy. Ordinary folk of Hokkien and Cantonese extraction flock to worship what is regarded as the people's deity, the enemy of injustice. For newlyweds, the Goddess is also identified with the Indian

---

Don't Overdo It

If you think the Khoo Kongsi is a shade too showy, you should have seen the original. In 1894 clan elders decided to put up a clan house that would rival in opulence China's imperial palace. It took eight years to complete and burned down on the night of its completion. Convinced that the deities had been offended by the extravagance of the building's design, the elders built the more 'modest' structure you see today.

Boddhisattva of Fertility. The shrine is protected by two stone lions at the entrance and guardian dragons on the roof. The atmosphere is heavy with the incense of burning joss-sticks mixed with the aroma of flowers, scented oils, fruits, cakes and roast chicken offered on the altars to help solve family problems. This is accompanied by the clicking of divining sticks to attract the busy deity's attention. Worshippers can also turn to images of the Laughing Buddha, Saviour of the Nether regions, God of War and Spirit of the White Tiger.

Also on the same street is the **Kapitan Kling Mosque**, originally erected for Muslim Indian soldiers of the 19th century.

Beyond the City Centre

Hugging the town's north shore, **Gurney Drive** assembles a colourful collection of open-air food courts where you can sample, among other delicacies, Penang's famous *laksa* noodles in hot shrimp or co-conut sauce and spicy *nasi kandar* rice with meat or fish.

Drive out along **Jalan Sultan Ahmad Shah** to see some of the finest of the rubber magnates' Neo-Gothic and Palladian mansions, built during the boom that lasted through World War I.

The funicular railway up Penang Hill affords spectacular views of the island.

The Thai Buddhist **Wat Chayamangkalaram monastery**, off Lorong Burma, is famous for its 33m (108ft) long reclining Buddha.

On the north-west outskirts of Georgetown, the **Penang Botanical Gardens** cover 30 hectares (74 acres) of jungle and hilly parkland cooled by sparkling waterfalls. The array of ferns and tropical flowers is quite remarkable. Star attractions among the wildlife are the dusky leaf monkeys and long-tailed macaques.

Jalan Dato Keramat then Jalan Ayer Hitam lead west of town to **Penang Hill**, 830m (2,722ft) tall, which served as a classical colonial hill station at the turn of the century. Take a delightful slow ride on the funicular railway (built in 1923), up past bungalows and villas set amid handsome gardens for a superb view of the island across to the mainland at the top. To escape the lowland heat, you can stay at the old Bellevue Hotel. Day trippers walk along trails through dense groves of bamboo and spot here and there the fascinating insect-eating pitcher plants (see p122). Birdwatchers look out for blue-tailed bee-eaters, sunbirds and spider-hunters.

Above the small town of Ayer Hitam stands the **Kek Lok Si**—Buddhist Temple of Paradise. It was founded in 1904 by Abbot Beow Lean, and set in hilly countryside that reminded him of his native Foochow in the south China province of Fukien. Its most spectacular feature is the seven-tiered **Pagoda of a Million Buddhas**, 30m (100ft) high. It is a synthesis of three styles of Buddhist architecture, since it consists of a Chinese octagonal base, a Thai central core and a Burmese peak. At the **Tortoise Pond**, visitors feed the creatures special vegetables and 'tortoise biscuits'. Boulders in the grounds are covered with Chinese writings of Buddhist and Confucian texts. Inside the shrine you will see statues of the Laughing Buddha, radiating happiness, Sakyamuni Buddha, incarnation of the faith's founder, and Kuan Yin, Goddess of Mercy.

Around the Island

Away from Chinese-dominated Georgetown, a tour around the island, covering about 74km (46 miles), will give you a better chance, as on the mainland, to meet the Malay population, based principally in the rural *kampongs* and fishing villages. The countryside varies between hilly rainforest and occasional plantations of rubber, oil palms, pepper groves, nutmegs, cloves and other spices, some of them originally planted a couple of centuries ago to attract Arab traders.

Driving west from Georgetown past the restaurants of Tanjung Tokong and the fishing cove of Tanjung Bungah, first stop—if you are not already staying there—is likely to be the popular bouncing beach resort of **Batu Ferringhi**. It is just what it means, 'Foreigner's

91

Rock', plus sandy beaches, luxury hotels and facilities for all imaginable water sports.

For fishing and snorkelling, head 6km (4 miles) west to Teluk Bahang and hire a boat out to **Muka Head** on the island's north-west tip. Alternatively, trek through the Pantai Acheh Forest Reserve.

One kilometre south of Teluk Bahang is a **Butterfly Farm** that boasts hundreds of different specimens fluttering around a netted enclosure of landscaped gardens.

The **Pantai Acheh Forest Reserve** covers some 20sq km (8sq miles) of the north-west corner of the island. There, you will find sandy beaches on the coast for camping, but no other form of accommodation. This may be strictly for nature-loving ramblers as motor vehicles are not allowed in, but it does reward visitors with a superb array of jungle trees, orchids and ferns. The wildlife includes wild pigs, leopard-cats (wild cats with leopard-spotted coats), slow loris, flying lemurs, leaf monkeys, macaques and black squirrels. The landscape is hill country dotted with granite outcrops.

For some inland freshwater swimming and fishing, try the natural pool fed by mountain waterfalls

Looking down on the small town of Ayer Hitam, Kek Lok Si's Pagoda of a Million Buddhas is a fascinating mix of architectural style.

at **Titi Kerawang**, 10km (6 miles) south of Teluk Bahang.

Stop off at any of the towns and *kampongs* that you pass as you drive south and enjoy the relaxed way of life of the Malays, a world apart from the Chinese bustle of Georgetown. **Balik Pulau** is famous for its pungent durian fruit. Birdwatchers gather around **Genting**, one of the world's largest nesting grounds for bee-eaters of all varieties—blue-tailed, blue-throated, chestnut-headed and others gather here in their hundreds.

As the road turns north again past the airport at Bayan Lepas, look out for signs to the **Snake Temple** or, more properly, Temple of the Azure Cloud. It was founded in 1873 by followers of the Taoist mendicant monk, Chor Soo Kong. After the temple was invaded by green and yellow pit vipers, it was decided that the snakes were incarnations of the monk and they were accorded sacred status. (The vipers multiply in impressive numbers during the monk's birthday month of July, but zoologists offer unmystical explanations.) In any case, they now infest various altars in the shrine where they are fed chicken eggs by the faithful. Although they do have a poisonous bite, they are said to be doped into a harmless state by the omnipresent incense smoke, while a few have had their teeth pulled to be photographed with tourists. An old Anglo-Saxon proverb says: 'You pays your money and takes your chance.'

93

NORTH TO LANGKAWI

Part of an archipelago of some 100 islets, the pretty resort island of Langkawi belongs to Kedah state but in fact lies off the coast of Perlis. If you are travelling there by road (rather than taking a flight from KL), ferries leave from the ports of Kuala Perlis and Kuala Kedah. There is also an overnight ferry from Penang.

The Kedah–Perlis Coast Road

From Butterworth, Penang's mainland railway junction, the road north passes by the **Bujang Valley**. Indian merchants settled there in ancient times, bringing their Hindu and Buddhist culture with them. Archaeologists are still uncovering remains on the southern slopes of **Gunung Jerai** (Kedah Peak), 1,200m (3,936ft) high.

Via the towns of Sungai Petani and Bedong, turn off left to **Merbok** to visit the **Candi Bukit Batu Pahat** (Temple of Chiselled Stone Hill), excavated beside a mountain stream. It was probably built by representatives of the South Indian Pallava dynasty before the 7th century BC. More artifacts, ceramics, *lingams,* stone caskets, and gold and silver Shiva symbols can be seen at Merbok's **Archaeological Museum**.

Fishermen's boats at the edge of the jungle, on Langkawi Island.

The flat countryside of Kedah's coastal plain is crisscrossed by **rice paddies** fed by the highly successful new Muda River irrigation system. In the state capital, **Alor Setar**, visit the sultan's grand **Balai Besar** (1898) built in Thai style for the royal audiences. Opposite the Zahir Mosque is the impressive octagonal **Balai Nobat**, a tower where the royal *nobat* drums, flutes and gongs are stored. Nobat, the royal orchestra, is played during royal ceremonies. The **State Museum** is worth a visit for its collection of *Bunga Mas* and *Bunga Perak* (flowers made of real gold and silver) which were sent to the Thai court as tribute.

At the nearby port of **Kuala Kedah**, you can see the remains of an 18th-century fort and sample some of the best seafood in northern Malaysia, especially crab. **Kuala Perlis** is a small fishing village near the Thai border where you can buy good cheap fruit at the local market for your ferry trip to Langkawi.

✅ Langkawi Island

The island is attempting a delicate balancing act between preserving its natural beauties and exploiting the economic potential of its resort facilities. At present, in addition to more modest accommodation near the beaches, there are five major luxury resort complexes—**Pelangi**, **Langkawi Island Resort**, **Burau Bay Resort**, **Sheraton Langkawi** and **Langkawi Holiday Villa**. The main town of **Kuah** has some good

Chinese, Thai, Indian and Malay restaurants and shops selling low-priced alcohol, cigarettes, perfume, crockery and designer clothes on this duty-free island.

To discover Langkawi's 80km (50 miles) of roads, the hotels rent out four-wheel-drive and standard cars, but many find bicycles and motorcycles the most attractive way to explore the island and reach the more secluded beaches.

Swimmers should be careful of powerful currents at most of the **beaches**. On the south-west corner of the island, try **Pantai Cenang** and the less crowded **Pantai Tengah**. On the west coast, **Pantai Kok** is beautifully set in a bay formed by jungle-clad limestone hills. Over on the north coast, to enjoy the (natural) black sands of **Pantai Pasir Hitam**, you must ignore the cement factory in the background.

As a change of pace from beach-lizarding, take a **jungle trek** across the middle of the island. Guided tours can be arranged for the hilly **Gunung Raya** and **Machinchang Forest Reserves**. Wildlife includes long-tailed macaques, dusky leaf monkeys, mouse-deers, wild pigs and giant squirrels. Birdwatchers are rewarded with stork-billed king-fishers and the most amenable of pied and rhinoceros hornbills. One of the easier walks takes you over to the **Durian Perangin Waterfall**.

For a little romantic folklore, visit **Mahsuri's Tomb**, 12km (7 miles) west of Kuah. A white marble monu-

A popular site with both locals and tourists: Mahsuri's Tomb.

ment set in a picturesque little garden pays tribute to a beautiful woman wrongfully executed for adultery. Before she died, she placed a curse on the island, sentencing it to seven generations without peace or prosperity. Since people cannot agree on when exactly she was executed, nobody knows whether the malediction has yet run its course.

Island hopping can be organized from Kuah or Pelangi. On **Pulau Dayang Bunting**, you can explore the **Gua Langsir bat cave**. It is believed to be haunted, so you may have trouble finding a guide or boat man to take you there. Barren Malaysians drink from the magic freshwater lake at the southern end of the island.

THE EAST COAST AND JOHOR

Having for centuries avoided the attentions of European merchants and colonizers and Chinese migrant labour, the peninsula's East Coast remains the last bastion of authentic Malay culture and Islam in its traditional forms. Resistance to the assaults of a burgeoning oil industry and modern commerce may be difficult, but handicrafts and old customs are still practised in many a rural *kampong* in the states of Kelantan and Terengganu.

At the same time, unspoiled sandy beaches are in much better shape than on the west coast. Wildlife enthusiasts can watch giant mother leatherback turtles laying their eggs or, later, watch baby turtles scampering—to the extent that a turtle can scamper—to the safety of the sea. Besides its beach resorts, Pahang, the peninsula's largest state, has an abundance of natural sites. They include the lotus-clad Lake Chini, the beautiful Tioman

Island and, straddling Pahang's border with Johor, the vast Endau-Rompin park. The southernmost state of Johor is linked by a causeway to Singapore, whose well-heeled tourists favour its resorts, first-class seafood restaurants and the nightclubs of its capital, Johor Bahru.

KELANTAN

White sandy beaches stretch north from the state capital, Kota Bharu, to the Thai border. To the south, fishing villages prevail. Inland, rice paddies occupy the plain until it gives way to rainforest. These can be explored on river safaris and jungle treks run by tour operators in Kota Bharu.

The pace of life in the fishing ports and country villages is much more relaxed than on the West Coast. The only thing approaching bustle is an occasional mix-up of trishaws at a road crossing in the state capital. Otherwise, you can safely slow down and take time to absorb the atmosphere of smiling market women and tranquil craftsmen.

Kota Bharu

The town serves principally as a springboard for exploring the East Coast but will also give you a feel for the authentic Islamic way of life, Malay style.

The market of Kota Bharu is one of the most thrilling courts in Malaysia.

Traditional boat-building takes place in Kelantan, as does the age-old craft of batik-painting.

A first surprise comes at Kota Bharu's major attraction, the **Pasar Besar** (Central Market) of spices, fruit, flowers and vegetables, one of the most colourful spots in all Malaysia. Under a glazed roof, galleries of hardware and textile shops rise in three tiers around the central space occupied by the food stalls. Climb to the top floor to look down on the kaleidoscopic display of green beans and ferns, pink lotus blossoms, yellow bananas and vermilion-red chilli peppers. Then come down again to wander among the stalls and you will see that in this supposedly male-dominated Islamic world the place is actually run by the women, dressed in colours as bright as their wares. The menfolk scurry around at their wives' bidding. Early in the morning you may witness the sale of the region's prized *merbuk* turtle-doves, nurtured to compete in singing competitions in surrounding villages, in addition to the 'championship' staged in Kota Bharu in June.

On the other side of the busy thoroughfare, Jalan Tok Hakim, is the sultan's palace audience hall, **Istana Balai Besar** (1844), its fine wood carvings still providing an elegant décor for royal weddings.

Crossing the Peninsula

The East Coast's unique atmosphere was for long preserved by the mountain barrier of the Main Range. Today, both Kelantan's Kota Bharu and Pahang's Kuantan are accessible by air or cross-country highways from KL or Penang. If you are coming in from Singapore, Tumpat, near Kota Bharu, is also served by train from Johor Bharu. Tour operators can arrange rental cars to explore the coast from the airports or railway station. Since East Coast Muslims are stricter in their religious observance, the holy month of Ramadan around March can pose problems for hotels and restaurants. Travel is also more difficult during the monsoon season from November to January.

Inside, you can see an ornate Royal Barge used just once by the sultan, in 1900, for a pleasure cruise on the nearby Kelantan River. Next door is the **Istana Jahar Palace**, housing the local craftsmanship of the **Kelantan State Museum** in another appropriately handsome setting of wood panelling and beautifully fashioned root beams.

Over towards the river, on Padang Merdeka (Independence Square), are the **State Mosque** and the venerable building of the **Hong Kong and Shanghai Banking Corporation** (1913), which served as the Japanese army headquarters in World War II. In the evening, the car park east of the square becomes an aromatic open-air **food court** for Malay and Chinese restaurants. You will find more at the **night market** opposite the bus station. About 100 metres behind the mosque is the newly opened handicraft centre, featuring a cluster of grand wooden buildings with ornate carved panels and pillars.

At the south end of town off Jalan Mahmood, the **Kelantan Cultural Centre** stages demonstrations of traditional sports and entertainments (see pp161–2): top-spinning, kite flying and the Malay martial art of *silat*, a kind of fencing. There

are also performances of *mak yong* dancing and *wayang kulit* puppet shadow plays (see pp154–5). For details of show times, inquire at the Tourist Information Centre on Jalan Sultan Ibrahim.

Around Kota Bharu

The maze of country lanes around Kota Bharu's hinterland may make it difficult for you to track down the *kampong* communities where artisans still practise the old traditional skills. Even if you do not want to hitch up with a tour group, we recommend that you take along an experienced tour guide. Kota Bharu's Tourist Information Centre will be able to help you out and recommend a suitable guide.

Kelantan silversmiths are renowned for their delicate artistry.

Kampong Sireh is known for its fine silversmiths, **Kampong Penambang** for its weavers of *Kain Songket* silk brocades and for its batik dyers. Elsewhere, you find old men—the younger generation lacks the patience—painstakingly glueing together coloured papers or flimsy transparent plastic over fragile bamboo frames to create a giant bird- or butterfly-kite. In these and other villages, look out, too, for people training their pet *merbuk* turtledoves to sing.

Kelantan's ancient links with Thailand just across the border are attested to by the number of **Thai Buddhist temples** you will see half hidden among groves of palm and laurel, rising above the rice paddies. North of the estuary of the Kelantan River at **Tumpat** is one of the most important, the **Wat Phothivihan** temple, noted for its giant reclining Buddha. At **Kampong Perasit**, south of Kota Bharu is the **Wat Putharamaram**.

From the eternity of Buddha's message to the bloody mortality of man's, visit **Sabak Beach**, 13km (8 miles) north-west of Kota Bharu near the mouth of the Kelamantan River, site of the first Japanese assault in the Pacific War, over an hour before Pearl Harbor was bombed in Hawaii (see p30). Jutting out of the sandy beach in the pleasant shade of palm and casuarina trees is the shell-scarred stone pillbox which the Indian artillery defended to the last man.

> **War on the Beach**
> *For their overland offensive through the peninsula to Singapore, the Japanese sent in a first wave of three troopships of 5,300 men just after midnight, on 8 December 1941. As the landing barges plunged through monsoon-whipped seas towards Sabak Beach, an escorting cruiser and three destroyers bombarded shore batteries manned by Indian soldiers of the 3/17th Dogra Regiment. Backed up by Australian and British pilots flying heavy Hudson and Vickers bombers, the coastal artillery succeeded in sinking two of the troopships. During the beach fighting, the Japanese lost one-third of their assault forces before overcoming the last defenders, who died rather than withdraw from their pillbox positions.*

The Beaches

Kelantan's white sandy beaches provide plenty of opportunities for a pleasant swim. Most popular is **Pantai Chinta Berahi**—meaning 'Beach of Passionate Love', a somewhat incongruous name in this strict Muslim region—situated 10km (6 miles) north of Kota Bharu. More secluded, **Pantai Kuda** ('Horse Beach') lies some 25km (15 miles) further north.

To the south, **Pantai Irama** ('Melody Beach') is 25km (15 miles) from Kota Bharu. On your way down to Terengganu, stop off at the fishing village of **Semerak**, 19km (12 miles) from Pasir Puteh, where you can buy excellent seafood for a barbecue on the beach at **Pantai Dalam Rhu**.

TERENGGANU

Business preoccupations since the discovery of offshore petroleum and natural gas have made little more than a ripple on Terengganu's easy-going style of life. This is particularly true in the fishing villages and on the many islands along the coast.

The Islands

Coming south on the main Kelantan–Terengganu highway, turn off at Pasir Puteh to the fishing village of **Besut**. The dockside market sells delicious deep-fried fish crackers, other seafood, fruit and vegetables for your picnic, and hand-woven beach mats. Fish trawlers and other boats will take you out to the islands. Two hours from the coast, **Pulau Perhentian Besar** offers fine unspoiled white sandy beaches

and superb snorkelling among the coral reefs.

The thatched-roof chalet accommodation has been upgraded whilst retaining its traditional appearance. Across a narrow channel is the baby sister island, **Perhentian Kecil**, boasting a tiny fishing village. The multicoloured marine life among the coral includes anemone fish, butterfly fish and long-spined angelfish.

A more remote island is **Pulau Redang**. It is accessible from the fishing village of Kampong Merang (not to be confused with the town of Marang further south) or Besut, and comes highly recommended by the diving fraternity. You will find a high-class resort with a golf course on this beautiful island.

(Left) Terengganu fishermen. (Below) A hard task: removing husks from coconuts.

105

Kuala Terengganu

The sleepy state capital, unperturbed by the bustle generated by oil activities further down the coast, is built on a promontory at the estuary of the Terengganu River. Its main street is the colourful **Jalan Bandar**. The Chinese are more in evidence here with shophouses and temples clustered around the inevitable clocktower. Tucked behind Jalan Bandar, **Dalam Kota** is a 'village-in-the-town', a maze of alleys lined with traditional Thai-style wooden houses. Notice the sturdy timbered tile-roofs and fine wood carving.

Along the riverbank, visit the **town market** (Pasar Besar). The fish is fresh from the docks and you will also find a rich array of chickens, fruit and vegetables.

From a jetty behind the taxi station, take a **river cruise**, which includes a visit to the boat builders on the little island of **Pulau Duyong**. The time-honoured skills of the craftsmen fashioning hardwood find few local customers these days. The clientele is more exclusive now—wealthy American and Australian yachtsmen.

Istana Maziah, the old royal palace on Jalan Pantai, is built somewhat in the style of a French country house. Behind it is the new **Zainal Abidin mosque**. For a good **view** of the town and out over the South China Sea, climb **Bukit Besar** hill at the southern end of town.

Some 7km (4 miles) further south on the road to Marang is a handsome traditional timbered Malay palace, **Istana Tengku Nik**, moved here from the city centre. However, the best place to see ancient Malay palaces is at Losong, a newly opened museum complex in Kuala Terenganu which houses several reconstructed palaces and a maritime museum.

Around Kuala Terengganu

Two villages where you will find the old handicrafts still going strong are **Rusila** for baskets and mats and **Kampong Tanjung** for brassware, batik dyeing and weaving of *Kain Songket* (silver or gold brocade).

Explore the jungle interior with an excursion to the beautiful **Sekayu Waterfalls**, 56km (35 miles) west of Kuala Terengganu. After trekking through the rainforest (avoid the easier route through the ugly recreation park), you will enjoy a swim in one of the many natural pools created among the rocks by the cascading river.

Marang is a fishing village 15km (9 miles) south of Kuala Terengganu. Here and across the long wooden bridge at **Patah Malam**, you may see fishermen peacefully mending their nets in the shade of coconut palms. One of them may be persuaded to take you out in his brightly

The crystal-clear waters of Malaysia's east coast are much sought-after by beach lizards and divers alike.

painted boat with a beautiful carved bow to the white sandy beaches of the pretty **Pulau Kapas** island, particularly appreciated for its snorkelling among tropical fish. You will find a couple of small chalets but no restaurants.

Rantau Abang

Even if the turtles were not there, Rantau Abang, 60km (37 miles) south of Kuala Terengganu, would be a great beach resort. But it has earned worldwide fame as one of the greatest gathering places of pregnant turtles ready to lay their eggs. The beach attracts four main species of turtle: the hawksbill, the common green, the Olive Ridley and, above all, the giant leatherback. From June to September, an 18km (11-mile) stretch of white sandy beach offers the wondrous sight of mother leatherbacks laying their eggs in the sand. Several weeks later, the same stretch of sand offers the no less wondrous sight of hatchlings emerging to start their precarious struggle down to their natural habitat in the sea.

In the years before ecological awareness put a stop to the onlookers' devastating insensitivity, the turtles' rendezvous was treated as a great popular spectacle. Crowds gathered in festive mood to build campfires on the beach, dance to the blare of transistors, photograph by blinding flashlight the turtles' night-time egg laying, even ride the backs of the giant leatherbacks and poke open their heavy-lidded eyes.

Human stupidity and sea pollution almost put a stop to this natural phenomenon. The annual number of leatherbacks visiting Rantau Abang declined from about 2,000 in the 1950s to barely a couple of hundred by the end of the 1980s, when Malaysia's fisheries department stepped in to protect the turtles. The public is still allowed to visit the beach during the egg laying and hatching season but officials are there to enforce proper behaviour —no flashlights, no fires and no music—and to keep people at a respectful distance from the nesting turtles.

Toils of a Turtle
The giant leatherback turtles grow to a weight of 250 to 550kg (550 to 1,210lb) on a diet of jellyfish. At 3m (nearly 10ft) in length, they are the largest turtles in the world. They make their way from temperate or even polar waters of the Atlantic and Pacific to lay their eggs in the warm sands of tropical beaches like Rantau Abang. Only adult females ever leave the sea and only then to lay their eggs.

Mother Leatherback crawls up the beach to dry sand, usually under the discreet cover of darkness. With her front flippers, she scrapes out a hollow and then, with her rear flippers, a deeper cavity, up to 50–80cm (20–30in) in depth. In this chamber, she lays from 80 to 150 eggs. She then carefully covers the nest with sand and returns to the sea.

The leatherback usually nests three to four times a season, at two-week intervals. The whole process takes about two hours. Lumbering up and down the beach is an arduous process, interrupted by frequent pauses to weep tears that wash the sand out of her eyes. Back in the sea, Mother Leatherback sheds her clumsiness along with the sand and glides away gracefully.

Hatching takes 50 to 60 days. For some reason, temperature determines sex, with eggs laid in warmer sands producing females and cooler sands producing males. Despite Mother Leatherback's precautions, crabs and birds may uncover the eggs and eat them. Survivors break out of their shells in a group and push up through the sand. They head for the lightest point in their field of vision: the horizon of the sea. Their scampering is just as often a deadly race against the attentions of predator birds.

The Turtle Information Centre just north of the Rantau Abang village will give you details of beach chalets available for the all-night vigil. Full moon and high tide are the most likely time for action, but there is no guarantee.

Tanjung Jara and Points South

Justly known as the leading beach resort on the East Coast, Tanjung Jara provides first-class facilities for water sports, tennis, squash and cycling. The handsome copper-coloured wooden structure of the sprawling hotel is modelled after a traditional Malay palace. But the restaurant does not match the resort's other high standards and many people prefer to go to the fishing port of **Dungun** to sample the excellent Chinese seafood.

A little further south but light-years away in spirit is the oil town of **Kerteh**, centre of Terengganu's petroleum industry. If power stations, oil tankers and pipelines, crude-oil bases and natural gas processing facilities are not your cup of tea, then hire a boat from Dungun to the remote island of **Pulau Tenggol**,

30km (18 miles) offshore, and go snorkelling among the angelfish.

PAHANG

The largest state in the peninsula also boasts the longest river, the 475km (296-mile) long Pahang. It has its share of fine beach resorts, including the renowned Tioman Island (though access by sea is from the port of Mersing in Johor). A large part of

Taman Negara (see pp74–7) is located in Pahang, which provides road access to the park headquarters from Kuantan. Its other natural beauties include Lake Chini and, shared with Johor, the Endau-Rompin nature reserve.

The Coast

Among the resorts and fishing ports, Club Méditerranée has set up its vacation complex at the attractive village of **Cherating**. You can find other cheaper chalets on the beach. From the estuary of the Ular River, site of the picturesque fishing village of **Kampong Sungai Ular**, take a boat out to **Pulau Ular** (Snake Island) for a quiet swim and picnic.

At another fishing village, **Beserah**, you can watch water buffaloes haul the fish-catch in wagons to the village market and over to the anchovy-salting factory. It also has an important batik centre beside the river, where the cloth is soaked as part of the dyeing process. You will find a pleasant beach nearby at **Batu Hitam**.

Kuantan

Built on fortunes made in the tin mines, the state capital is now the commercial centre for Pahang's oil palm and other industries and an

Cherating–the holiday resort par excellence–harbours heavenly beaches to get away from it all.

important link in the East Coast petroleum and gas pipelines. What the town lacks in charm and colour, it makes up for in practicality. Kuantan is an ideal base for exploring the natural beauties of the interior, with first class hotels in its airy suburban beach resort of **Telok Cempedak**. A bizarre feature of the Hyatt hotel is the Sampan Bar, made out of a Vietnamese boat-people's vessel that was stranded on the nearby beach. You will find handicraft shops downtown along the busy main street, **Jalan Besar**. The local village of **Selamat** is known for its fine *Kain Songket* silk brocade.

Pekan

The sleepy old royal capital of Pahang, 45km (28 miles) south of Kuantang, is still the sultan's official residence. Upstream on the Pahang River, the sultan's gleaming palace, **Istana Abu Bakar** is set amid immaculate green polo fields. Gilded and sapphire-blue domes grace two white marble **mosques** and the **sultan's mausoleum**. Nearby, the old Victorian **state museum** displays glories of the old sultanate and treasures of a Chinese junk salvaged from the South China Sea.

Lake Chini

Chini in fact comprises a dozen beautiful lakes surrounded by densely forested hills south of the Pahang river, 56km (35 miles) west of Kuantan. From June to September, much of their surface is covered by white and red lotus blossoms. The myth-shrouded lakes are also said to be the home of giant snakes, dragons and other monsters, one of which swam out to the South China Sea to become Tioman Island. Some tour operators try to promote the presence of a fire-breathing Loch-Ness-like monster with red eyes— more probably the headlamps of a backfiring motorboat. More seriously, archaeologists are exploring the depths for the submerged remains of a Cambodian settlement.

If you prefer your own transport to a guided tour organized from Kuantan, take the Kuantan–Kuala Lumpur road to the 74km (46-mile) marker and turn off south for another 27km (16 miles) to the Pahang River. Hire a boat at Kampong Belimbing for a leisurely cruise beneath the shady tree canopy of the narrow **Chini River**. From time to time, the boatman may point out tracks made by elephants and other wild animals. Kingfishers swoop over the water in a flash of blue. Along the river banks, strangling figs are performing their splendid dastardly deeds, squeezing the life out of even the tall buttress-rooted tualang trees.

Outside the lotus-blossom season, the lakes are still a delight to visit, offering good fishing for the much appreciated local *toman*. Members of the local Jakun tribe dwelling on the lakeshore still use blowpipes to hunt monkeys and other wildlife. They supplement their diet by gathering

the protein-rich lotus seeds. Pay a discreet visit to one of their hamlets, **Kampong Gumum**.

Tioman Island

The combination of first-rate resort facilities and magnificent natural beauties makes Tioman one of the finest islands in Asia. Preserved from logging, most of the rainforest has remained in blissfully virgin state. A hilly ridge runs down the middle of the island at an altitude of 500m (1,640ft), rising at the southern end to two granite peaks—'Donkey's Ears'—the taller of which, Mount Kajang, is 1,038m (3,405ft) high.

You can reach Tioman by flying from Kuantan or by taking the boat from the fishing port of **Mersing** in Johor. The 'slow boat' and the 'fast boat' both end up taking three to four hours, so just sit back and work on your suntan.

On the island's west coast, you have the choice between the top-class **Tioman Island Resort Hotel** and more modest but perfectly comfortable guest-houses, chalets and simpler cabins on **Salang Beach** further north. Facilities around the main island port of **Tekek** include a **golf course**, where long-tailed macaques act as unofficial caddies who do not always give you your ball back.

Intrepid explorers and nature lovers trek in the Kenyir lake area of Terengganu.

Most of your trips around the island will be by boat, and the fishermen are very obliging, for a quite reasonable fee. From Tekek, make the **jungle trek** over the hill to the east coast. Cool off on the way with a dip at the hilltop waterfall and then make your way down to the beach at **Juara**, a village serving excellent seafood and banana pancakes. Take another swim in the sea and, if you do not feel like trekking back, return to Tekek by boat.

Birdwatchers will see green or pied imperial pigeons, bulbuls, frigate birds, sunbirds and flower-peckers. Characteristically for island-forests, there are no large mammals but you may spot mouse-deers, slow loris, macaques and flying lemurs.

Hollywood chose Tioman as the idyllic location for its musical comedy, *South Pacific*, and near **Mukut** at the southern tip of the island you can see the waterfall where Mary Martin decided to 'wash that man right out of my hair'.

JOHOR

The state rounds off the southern end of the peninsula. After providing a refuge in the 16th century for the Melaka sultanate and becoming the principal guardian of Malay culture, Johor, stimulated by its dynamic next-door neighbours in Singapore, has become one of the most modern states in the Federation. Its network of roads and railway links the bustling city of Johor Bahru to the East Coast and to KL on the West

Coast. In cooperation with Pahang, the otherwise impenetrable jungle of the interior is being carefully opened up as part of the Endau-Rompin nature reserve (named after two of its rivers). New beach resorts are being developed on the south-east coast around Desaru.

The Endau-Rompin Nature Reserve

The reserve embraces two state parks straddling the Pahang–Johor border and covering a surface of 800sq km (over 2,000sq miles). At the headwaters of the Endau River, the rugged forest country (for the most part peaty swamp heath forest) is surrounded by hills with dramatic waterfalls.

Much less developed than Taman Negara or the parks of Sarawak and Sabah—and so more pristine—Endau-Rompin is a splendid challenge to the adventurous visitor, but an experienced tour guide is essential. Camping is the only form of accommodation and you must bring your own food. You journey by boat from the coast at Endau, 37km (23 miles) north of Mersing, or by car from Kuala Rompin (Pahang) to a boat on the Kinchin River to reach base camp at **Kuala Jasin**, at the confluence of the Endau and Jasin rivers. You will make your way with *orang hulu* jungle guides in dugouts and canoes made of bark bound with rattan twine. When the waters are too shallow for easy progress, you will wade out to push.

Desaru

The south-east corner of the peninsula was originally exploited only for oil-palm plantations. Today, this fast-growing resort complex is catering to the water sports and yachting fraternity, as well as golfers from Singapore and Japan. Its high class hotels share 25km (15 miles) of golden sands.

On your way to or from Desaru, it's worth stopping off at **Kota Tinggi** and driving 15km (9 miles) north-east to its spectacular **waterfall** which plunges 36m (118ft) into the river below. It is illuminated after dark, and you can lodge in Swiss-style chalets and sample some good Chinese food at the restaurant facing the cascade.

Johor Bahru

Citizens of prosperous but rather staid Singapore (see pp140–6) cross the causeway to Johor's state capital to sample its bouncing nightlife watered by cheaper alcohol. There is little to keep the overseas visitor. Drive along the **Lido seafront**, take a look at the gleaming white marble **Sultan Abu Bakar Mosque** and stroll in the **Istana Gardens** of the old palace, with its Japanese tea-house and zoo constituted from the sultan's private menagerie.

The Neo-Classical **Istana Besar palace** is now used only for state ceremonies, the present-day sultans having moved up the coast to the modern **Istana Bukit Serene** with its flashy 32m (104ft) high tower.

North Towards Melaka

A popular stopover for northbound travellers is **Ayer Hitam**. Besides its cafés and restaurants, the fruit market is much appreciated for the excellent rambutans, pineapples and bananas and locally made nougat and fruit-cakes. The town is also known for its gaudy **pottery**, displayed in breathtaking abundance near the fruit market.

Before heading towards Melaka and KL, gourmets coming from Johor Bahru turn off west at Sekudai to the coast road and back south to **Kukup**. If we are to believe the Singaporean epicures who regularly make the pilgrimage, this Chinese village of wooden houses on stilts linked by raised boardwalks serves the peninsula's best chilli crabs,

A bewildering range of potteries awaits you at the Ayer Hitam market.

mussels, prawns and sweet-and-sour fish. But you can also turn off at Ayer Hitam to the market town of **Batu Pahat**, which offers some very respectable Chinese restaurants. The town witnessed a historic Melaka naval victory over the Thai fleet in 1456. The fishing port of **Muar** was of trading importance to the British in the 19th century, as can be seen in the graceful old Neo-Classical government offices. It was also the scene of the Australian troops' heroic but abortive last stand against the Japanese advance on Singapore in January 1942.

115

SARAWAK AND SABAH

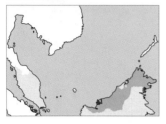

Borneo. The name has miraculously not lost its romantic magic. The natural wonders of the third largest island in the world, which the two states of East Malaysia share with Indonesia and the sultanate of Brunei, are sorely tried by the modern onslaughts of oil drilling, voracious logging of lucrative *belian* hardwood, and of tourism itself. But adventure is still possible in the virgin rainforests, caves and mountains of the northern interior and among the coral reefs of the South China Sea.

In Sarawak and Sabah, where the aboriginal populations still outnumber the Malays, Chinese and Indians, you can take a jungle river cruise to visit tribesmen in their forest homes. Or you may like to explore Sarawak's Niah Caves, with their ancient wall-paintings and madcap bird's-nest hunters. If you are feeling even more adventurous, tackle the tougher gigantic caves and granite pinnacles of the Mount

Mulu National Park. In Sabah, the Mount Kinabalu National Park attracts nature lovers and amateur climbers while, to the south, the Sepilok wildlife sanctuary offers a unique close-up of our orang-utang ancestors. For a change of pace, there are plenty of beaches along the northern and eastern coasts and plenty of islands for snorkelling or turtle-watching.

One of the factors to have preserved East Malaysia's tourist attractions is the difficulty of getting around the country by road. Few roads are paved and frequent rains make the others treacherously risky. The rivers, more numerous and much longer than on the peninsula, still provide the principal way into the interior, supplemented by a small aircraft operated by Malaysia Airlines. To go some place, you have to be really motivated and so more respectful of what you will see when you get there. If, after a long working year, you find yourself craving for the easy life, then just relax and stick to the beach.

SARAWAK

Malaysia's largest state—124,967sq km (48,250sq miles)—also boasts the longest river, the Rejang, flowing 563km (351 miles) from the mountains on the Indonesian border to the South China Sea. Along the Rejang and the Sarawak River and their myriad tributaries, you can visit the tribes of the rainforest and stay

Aborigines of Northern Borneo

In the old days, colonial officials and romantic novelists lumped together Borneo's aborigines as Land or Sea Dayaks. With the resurgence of ethnic pride, the people have reclaimed their individual tribal names: Iban, Melanau, Bidayuh, Kayan and Kenyah in Sarawak or Kadazan, Bajau, Murut and Kelabit in Sabah—plus Punan nomads ignoring state frontiers.

Some have assimilated the beliefs of Islam or Christianity, but the powerful presence of tropical nature has sustained a parallel allegiance to traditional animism. A couple of days in the Borneo jungle and you, too, will sense divine spirits in the trees.

Iban, the largest indigenous group in Sarawak comprising 30 per cent of the population, dwell in longhouses along lowland river banks. They live from dry-rice cultivation (as opposed to the more prevalent method of flooded paddies) and small-holdings of rubber and pepper. The last head-hunters have gone into retirement, but some of the severed heads—relics of the World War II campaign against the Japanese—are still hanging around their homes as mementos.

Melanau inhabit the coastal plain east of Kuching where they fish and grow raw sago. Many still supplement their Muslim or Christian beliefs with a medicine of 'sickness images': dolls carved from sago pith, representing the evil spirits causing the disease.

Bidayuh, the original Land Dayaks who allied with the White Rajas of the 19th century, are longhouse dwellers of western Sarawak. They practise dry-rice cultivation and make fine musical instruments—flutes, harps and gongs.

Kenyah and **Kayan** are two distinct tribes but often live side by side along the upper reaches of Sarawak's Baram and Rejang rivers. They farm hill rice and rubber and rear pigs and poultry. They are also renowned craftsmen, making anything from delicate hornbill-ivory earrings and finely carved wooden statues to the sturdiest of boats and longhouses.

Punan, the last of East Malaysia's nomads, stay upriver well clear of civilization, though you may hire one as a jungle guide in Mount Mulu National Park. The men make superb weapons—machetes and blowpipes—and the women are renowned as basket-weavers.

Kadazan, Sabah's biggest tribe, have adapted smoothly to urban life—and Christianity—in Kota Kinabalu. Others farm rice in the valleys and market vegetables on terraced hills around Mount Kinabalu.

Bajau are Muslim sailors affectionately known as Sea Gypsies, though some are feared for perpetuating the ancestral tradition of piracy. Their land-lubber cousins are similarly held in awe for their daring exploits as cowboy cattle-breeders.

Murut are fierce hunters in the hill country along the Sabah–Sarawak border, happily picking up their blowpipes when they run out of rifle ammunition. The Allies were glad to have them on their side during World War II.

117

overnight in their longhouses. Between your river cruises or treks through the rainforest of Bako National Park, you can relax on the beaches of Santubong and Damai outside Kuching or on the coast of Bako itself. In eastern Sarawak you can pursue more strenuous but exhilarating adventures among the Niah or Mulu caves, a far cry from the white sands and coconut palms favoured by the beach-lizards.

(Do not be surprised when you are subjected to immigration formalities on arriving in Sarawak. These are meant to protect the state against a flood of migrant labour from the peninsula or neighbouring Indonesia and the Philippines.)

Kuching

Unlike the other major towns of East Malaysia—Miri, Kota Kinabalu or Sandakan—Sarawak's state capital has preserved its old colonial charm, having been spared the bombs of World War II. Kuching is built on a bend in the Sarawak River, 32km (20 miles) from the sea. The residence and fort built by the Brooke dynasty of White Rajahs (see pp26–7) share the north bank with a string of riverside Malay kampongs, while most of the government buildings, the Chinese and Indian

Catcall
The town's name is said to have been given it by James Brooke, the first White Rajah, when a cat, kuching *in Malay, ran across the room during a conference with local chiefs. The legend has been enough to justify a whole room being given over to cats at the Sarawak Museum and a leading nightclub calling itself 'Cat City'.*

From Kuching, take the ferry across the river to the Malay kampongs and Fort Margherita.

merchants are situated on the south bank. The colonial buildings include the **Courthouse**, the **General Post Office** and the dungeon-like **Round Tower** that now serves as the Judiciary department.

To get a feel for the town, it is a good idea to start with a short **cruise** along the waterfront in a fisherman's canoe or on one of the *Tambang* ferries moored at **Pangkalan Batu** near the Main Bazaar. All day long the river is alive with trawlers, pole-punted longboats, steel-bottomed motor launches, *sampan* canoes and an occasional loose raft of logs from upriver timber camps. The latter are increasingly rare, as Sarawak's road transportation has improved and logging is restricted.

Take the ferry across to visit the Malay kampongs and **Fort Margherita**, built in 1841. This mock castle complete with medieval battlements and tower was named after Rajah Charles Brooke's wife, Margaret. It now houses a **Police Museum**. The collection of weapons on display includes material from the Japanese Occupation and a cannon cast locally for use against rebel pirates, though it wasn't fired from the fort itself. The Chamber of Laughing Skulls displays heads hunted by the Iban going back 200 years. The only laugh ever heard was that of the Iban entrepreneur who sold the skulls to the museum, claiming that they somehow managed to chuckle about their grisly fate.

Further west, **Astana** (1870), the Brookes' home and now the Governor of Sarawak's official residence, comprises three bungalows shaded by broad shingle roofs, set European-style among green lawns. Charles Brooke also kept a small betel nut garden in the grounds to supply visiting tribal chiefs with their favourite narcotic.

South of the river on Jalan Tun Haji Openg, **Sarawak Museum** has one of the best collections of folk art, flora and fauna in South-East Asia. It was created in 1888 by Charles Brooke and the naturalist Alfred Russel Wallace, but the architectural design of the original building, an attractive hybrid of French Normandy town hall and American colonial mansion, is attributed to Brooke's valet. A modern extension has been added across the street.

Highlights in the museum include a reconstructed **Iban longhouse**, complete with totem-pole, chieftains' beautiful hornbill-feather headdresses and skulls of head-hunting victims; **Kenyah Tree of Life mural** repainted from a longhouse original at Long Nawang; **Melanau dolls** serving as lucky charms against disease; **Hindu and Buddhist sculptures**; Chinese, Thai, Japanese and European **ceramics** and **brassware**; a model of the **Niah Caves** (see pp125–7), with their birds, bats and other fauna, Stone Age artifacts and funeral boats from the 8th century AD; part of **Wallace's insect collection**—2,000 species

---

Nature Sleuth

A contemporary of Charles Darwin, Alfred Russel Wallace proved a true detective in his pioneering research in evolution theory and 'biogeography', the geographical distribution of animals. In Malaysia, he is best known as the 'discoverer' of the national butterfly, the green and black 'Rajah Brooke Birdwing'. But his most intriguing contributions came in the field of natural mimicry. Beyond the familiar camouflage techniques of chameleons and stick-insects, he watched viceroy butterflies trick birds by cultivating a resemblance to the monarch butterfly that birds hate. And he discovered ant-eating spiders that look like ants.

found just around Kuching—as well as reptiles, birds, mammals and sea shells.

And, depending on your mood, you may choose to visit the **Petroleum Gallery** and technology section devoted to Sarawak's modern industries, or the **Cat Gallery** celebrating Kuching's mascot in all its guises—from Egyptian divinity to Fritz, Tom and Garfield. There is a high quality museum **gift shop**.

The modern **Civic Centre**, towering above a **Planetarium** and **Art Gallery**, gives a fine view over the town to the South China Sea. You can see the new green-domed **state mosque** built to hold a congregation of 8,000, supplementing the old but prettier sprawling white marble mosque with golden domes at the north end of Jalan Masjid.

The town has three major Chinese temples: the oldest, **Tua Pek Kong** (1876), on Jalan Padungan, **Hong San** at the corner of Jalan Carpenter and Jalan Wayang, and the popular **Kwan Yin** on Jalan Tabuan. The **Indian Mosque** between Lebuh India and Jalan Gambier stands at the centre of the Indian quarter of shops and restaurants.

The **Main Bazaar** is along the riverfront, but look out, too, for the **Pasar Dayak** (Dayak Market) near the old state mosque where Bidayuh farmers bring in their fruit and vegetables. Most colourful of all is the **Sunday Market** along Jalan Satok. In keeping with Muslim custom, this in fact starts on Saturday night and presents, in addition to the usual farm produce, a bewildering array of lizards, bats, monkeys, turtles and wild boar—a whiff of the wilderness in the city.

Around Kuching

A one-hour cruise by express-boat from Kuching to the delta of the Sarawak River will lead you to the fishing village of **Santubong**. There, you will find a fine beach for picnics and swimming and, if you care to go fishing, the fishermen will take you out with them for a modest fee. Hindu and Buddhist stone sculptures and artifacts found 1.5km (1 mile) up the Jaong tributary show that the delta was frequented over 1,000 years ago by Indian and Chinese traders.

The region is even more easily explored from the neighbouring **Damai resort**, whose long sandy beaches are set against a dramatic mountain backdrop. For a compact view of Sarawak's folklore, visit the **Sarawak Cultural Village**. Tribal houses and workshops are nicely laid out in a park, next to the hotel, and there are regular cultural shows.

At the western end of the coast road, the secluded fishing village of **Sematan** offers simple chalet accommodation from which to trek around the **Samunsan Nature Reserve**. You can also visit a nearby **crocodile refuge** or cruise around **turtle sanctuaries** out in the islands.

Semonggok, 22km (13 miles) inland from Kuching, is a rainforest rehabilitation centre for orang-utans. The scale is more modest than in Sepilok (see pp138–9) but it still gives you the opportunity to take a close-up look at our ancestor apes. Your best chance to see them is during their breakfast, 8 a.m.—early but the best time to be in the jungle—or late lunch, 3 p.m. The menu is water-melons, bananas, papayas or green beans. Hornbills, leaf monkeys, macaques and the occasional honey bear also hang around.

Bako National Park

The park is situated on a peninsula north of Kuching, from where it is easily accessible. In a small area of just 27sq km (10sq miles), you will be able to see a wide variety of rainforest types—mangrove, dipterocarp and heath (see pp44–7)—where botanists have distinguished 25 distinct forms of vegetation. Among the abundant wildlife, you will have a rare chance to see the famous proboscis monkey. And there is the added attraction of several delightful **beaches** for relaxation between your forays into the forest.

From Kuching, the bus takes 40 minutes or the ferry two hours (from the Long Wharf by Jalan Gambier) to Kampong Bako at the mouth of the Sarawak River. Here, a longboat transports you in 30 minutes to the park headquarters at Telok Assam. No vehicles are allowed inside the park. Accommodation is in comfortable rest houses or hostels, or you can camp on the nearby beaches.

The Meanest Pitcher in the Big League

The pitcher plant (see opposite page) consists of a bowl often shaped like a miniature tuba with a curved lid sticking upright when open. Why do insects fall in? Those that go for the nectar under the pitcher lid get away safely. Others going for the nectar glands under the pitcher's rim fall into a digestive liquid mixture of rainwater and enzymes. Unable to climb back up the sticky, scaly interior, they drown and the plant slowly digests them. Cashing in on the activity around these plants, some spiders spin webs across the inside of the pitcher's mouth and catch the falling insects.

The giant of the species is the Nepenthes rajah, with one pitcher measuring a record 46cm (18in) and holding 4 litres (7 pints) of water. These big guys have been found digesting frogs and even rats.

Jungle Trails

The park offers 16 well marked colour-coded paths with bridges over the swamps to the best spots for viewing the flora and wildlife, such as the **Lintang salt lick**. Immediately around **Telok Assam** you may see bearded pigs, mouse-deers and, at night, flying lemurs flitting from tree to tree. Besides its good hilltop view over the jungle, **Bukit Tambi** offers several specimens of carnivorous plants: the bladderwort, pitcher plant and sundew—also known as Venus's fly-trap.

Telok Delima and **Telok Paku** are the best places for viewing the proboscis monkey. You will recognize him, of course, by his telltale nose, but also by his big belly and brownish-orange fur. He likes to bed down in a tree near the sea-shore. Very often, he will have been quietly watching you long before you spot him and if your presence upsets him, he will just honk and disappear. While at the sea-shore, keep a look out, too, for the equally handsome hairy-nosed otter.

Birdwatchers can notch up over 150 species, including migrant terns, sandpipers and plovers. Blue flycatchers and magpie robins hang around the park HQ, and reef egrets, sunbirds and kingfishers by the water.

The Beaches

Out on the Bako peninsula, bays of white sandy beaches are backed by beautiful sheer cliffs clothed in stunted mangrove and ferns. The nearest is at **Telok Assam** itself. **Telok Paku** is a 45-minute walk from the park HQ, **Telok Pandan Kecil** 90 minutes away. But you can also seek out more secluded spots in little creeks you would prefer to keep nameless.

Longhouse River-Cruises

The opportunity to see the tribes of Sarawak in their forest homes is a privilege not to be squandered. You will share meals with the families, toast each other with a heady swig of *tuak*, a sweet wine made from glutinous rice, see **tribal dances**, watch craftsmen at work. You will be shown traditional **hunting** methods, and may learn to use a **blowpipe**. On longer stays you may go on a **fishing** expedition. The most rewarding experience of all is quite simply to be taken on a walk in the forest and see it through the eyes of its inhabitants. (It is the custom, as a guest of the tribe, to bring gifts—cigarettes, sweets, little toys for the children.)

But you must also steer clear of the fake atmosphere of longhouse villages sadly corrupted by over-commercialized mass tourism. Let the Malaysian tourist authorities advise on reputable tour operators in Kuching who organize visits on a small scale not offensive to tribal dignity.

It is not possible to name from one year to the next which river excursion you should choose, as each tour operator favours a particular longhouse community along the Rejang or Sarawak rivers or its tributaries. Beware of some, like the much touted Skrang River Adventure, for instance, which have acquired the artificial character of a 'tribal theme park'. The little gifts are regarded practically as payment, the dances are perfunctory and without charm, the craftsmanship demonstrated only in the expectation of selling the products.

The excursion usually involves a three- or four-hour road journey to the river and then a one-hour

In the Longhouse

A typical longhouse is a communal dwelling of perhaps 20 'apartments', attached one to the other and prolonged as each extended family adds a unit of parents with children. Erected close to the river, it is built of sturdy axe-hewn timber, preferably Sarawak's coveted belian ironwood, tied with liana fibre and roofed with palm-frond thatching. The structure is raised above the ground on massive pillars—a technique evolved in the past to resist enemy attacks rather than mere river flooding.

A notched tree trunk serves as a stairway to the outer open verandah, where the families congregate, dry their washing or lay out their fish, spices, fruit, nuts and vegetables. On the inner closed verandah are the communal 'lounges', kept for recreation and ceremonies.

Off to the side behind partitions, family dwellings consist of bedrooms and kitchens. An attic under the roof is used for hoarding grain or rice, often stored in giant earthenware jars bought from the Chinese. The attic sometimes doubles up as a weaving-room.

Modern times have brought running tap-water, electricity generators, cooking stoves, radio and television, whilst some tribesmen proudly display banners of British football clubs and pin-ups of Hollywood stars. But they also cling to their traditions, wearing sarongs and proudly bearing hornbill tattoos on their throat and arms. Hanging from pillars and rafters beside the quartz clock are the ancestral head-hunting trophies—believed to give the clan strength and good fortune.

cruise by longboat. Occasionally, on stretches where the river is low, you may be asked to wade in the shallows and help push the boat into navigable waters—an exercise that is more refreshing than risky.

Immediately around Kuching, you are most likely to visit a long house of the **Iban** tribe, perhaps on the **Lemanak River**. To the east, you can visit the **Kenyah** and **Kayan** tribes (see p117). Excursions are organized either via Miri from Kuala Baram along the **Baram River** or, via Sibu, from Kapit or Belaga up the **Rejang River**. The approach to Belaga entails a bracing passage through the Rejang's **Pelagus**

Rapids. There are seven in all, each with its own name: *Bidai* (big mat), *Nabau* (python), *Lunggak* (dagger), *Pantu* (sago), *Sukat* (measure), *Mawang* (fruit) and most ominously *Rapoh* (tomb).

Niah Caves

The caves were the home of Malaysia's earliest traces of *homo sapiens*. Later, they were used as burial grounds for nomadic tribesmen and now as the hunting-ground of daredevil collectors of cave-roof bird's nests.

The Niah excursion starts out from **Miri**—the birthplace of Sarawak's oil industry. Though most of the drilling activity has moved west to Bintulu and offshore, you can still see where Shell drilled the first oil well in 1910 on **Canada Hill**, overlooking the town. Miri is almost entirely modern in aspect after the British and Dutch blew up all the oil installations in 1941 rather than let them fall into the hands of the Japanese.

For your cave tour, be sure to take a powerful torch (flashlight), sturdy walking shoes with a good grip, and leave a change of shirt and socks in the car—the humidity is quite intense. On a day trip, a 2-hour drive

---

All That for a Bowl of Soup?

Descendants of the nomadic Punan tribesmen who rediscovered the Niah Caves' bird's-nest riches in the 19th century divide up the cave into jealously guarded 'stakes', handed down from father to son. To scrape the nests from the cave ceiling, the Punan climb more than 60m (200ft) up a series of swaying bamboo poles tied together, or through narrow 'chimneys' inside the rock. As the old song says, 'A lotta men did and a lotta men died'—nobody knows how many.

White-bellied swiftlets are responsible for the high-priced nets, made from pure saliva rendered particularly glutinous by a diet of algae. An inferior product is furnished by 'black-nest' swiftlets who mix feathers in with the saliva. To the dismay of Western gourmets, the Chinese insist that the viscous, translucent soup is worth the trouble.

---

along unpaved road takes you to **Batu Niah** for lunch and from there to the Niah National Park headquarters at **Pangkalan Lubang**. Here you obtain a permit and take the ferry across the Niah River to a pleasant 4km (2.5 miles) boardwalk path through the jungle to the cave entrance.

On the way, notice half-hidden among the trees the strange limestone rock formations that look like medieval ramparts. If you arrive early, you might spot mouse-deer, pig-tailed macaque monkeys, hornbills and bulbuls or even catch a rare glimpse of the colourful trogons.

The main or **Great Cave** is a hollow 400m (1,312ft) up in the sandstone Subis plateau. Besides some giant crickets and scorpions (from which the extension of the boardwalk through the cave keeps you safe), the cave is home to millions of bats and swiftlets. Their daily droppings furnish one ton of highly valued guano fertilizer. In 1958, a curator of Kuching's Sarawak Museum dug down through the mounds of guano and found at a depth of 2.4m (8ft) fragments of a 40,000-year-old skull, the earliest physical relics of *homo sapiens* in South-East Asia. The fragments of Deep Skull, as it is known, together with tools, earthenware pots, jars and later bronze jewellery found nearby are displayed in the Kuching museum.

But more lucrative than the guano are the swiftlets' edible nests for which Chinese merchants from

Singapore, Hong Kong and Shanghai are prepared to pay hundreds of dollars per kilo (100 nests), reselling them for thousands, to make the gourmet delicacy of bird's nest soup. You can watch Punan tribesmen collecting the nests all year round, but April–May and September–October are the optimal seasons. Park authorities impose a quota system to limit the threat to the swiftlets' survival.

The swiftlets and bats share the cave on separate day and night shifts. At dusk, you can see the birds return round about the time that the bats go out for dinner. This flurry of 'rush hour' traffic, involving hundreds of thousands of bats and birds, is an astonishing spectacle. Another wonder is how each bird manages to get back to its right nest. Not all the bats get back—some crested goshawks and bat-hawks are waiting outside the cave to pounce.

The boardwalk continues through the Great Cave down to the **Painted Cave**. Discovered in 1958 at the same time as Deep Skull, its wall-paintings representing red stick-figures of spread-eagled dancers were executed in a mixture of betel juice and lime around AD 700. The cave probably served as a burial chamber: canoe-coffins were also found here (on show in the Sarawak Museum). Other relics seem to indicate that these Niah people traded swiftlets' nests and hornbill ivory for Chinese porcelain and beads and were perhaps the direct ancestors

of the Punan themselves—giving the present day bird's-nest collectors a certain proprietary claim.

Mount Mulu National Park

This newly developed park, which covers 528sq km (204sq miles) of spectacularly craggy terrain along the Melinau River in eastern Sarawak, is a quite demanding adventure, best tackled by the fit and tough. For an expedition of at least four to five days, a tour operator is essential—to take care of permits and supply experienced guides, usually members of the Punan tribe. The best guides will provide miner's helmets with built-in lamps to explore the pitch-black caves. Your own equipment should include very strong shoes, made of rubber rather than leather, lots of socks, tough old clothes, a pair of gloves and a light sleeping bag.

The rewards are magnificent. The **gigantic caverns** in the mountain's sheer cliffs are reputed to be the largest in the world. Around them, torrents plunge into fathomless gorges. Only experienced climbers tackle **Mount Mulu**, 2,376m (7,793ft) high, but trekking through the virgin rainforest is superb. The park's other great attraction are the **limestone pinnacles**, soaring above the trees halfway up the slopes of Mount Api.

From Miri (see p125), travel by road to Kuala Baram on the coast and then by boat up the Baram River to **Marudi**. A second boat takes you on the Tutuh River with local

127

lumberjacks and tribesmen via **Long Terawan** to the park headquarters at the confluence of the Melinau. (The all-day journey can be shortened a few hours by flying from Miri to Marudi or Long Lalang.)

The Caves

There are two main 'show caves' and countless other 'wild caves' which are either too dangerous or ecologically too fragile to visit without special permits and qualified guides. In any case, expect some crawling around on hands and knees or wading chest-deep through underground streams. Mulu is not for claustrophobes.

To give you an idea of the scale of these caverns, **Sarawak Chamber**, the most recently explored cave and not yet open to the public, is said to be as big as 16 football fields or to be large enough to provide hangar-space for 40 jumbo jets.

For an easy start, take the pleasant forest walk to **Deer Cave**. Its vast entrance hall has three waterfalls and a ceiling 190m (623ft) high. Its passage is 2km (1.5 miles) long. Climb down the rope-ladder to the **Garden of Eden**, a hidden green valley of tropical vegetation.

A troglodytes' paradise, **Clearwater Cave** has been measured as 51km (31 miles) long. After you have waded and crawled for about three hours with only your lamps to illuminate the cave's total darkness, a hole in the cave-roof brings in a sudden burst of sunlight to reveal the greenery it has nurtured here over the centuries. From there on, it is all black.

Exploring the **Pinnacles**, 900m (3,000ft) up the side of Mount Api, may add a couple of days to the expedition, but there are few sights to match these gigantic stone needles thrusting like petrified hooded ghosts above the dark green canopy of the forest. A bonus for amateur botanists are the ten varieties of pitcher plant they can log on the way, while birdwatchers may spot eight different kinds of hornbill.

As at Niah, crested goshawks and bat-hawks wait at the cave entrances for the bats' twilight excursion. Other birds among Mulu's 260 recorded species include stork-billed kingfishers, myna birds and strawheaded bulbuls. Look out, too, for gibbons, martens, honey bears and pygmy squirrels.

SABAH

Covering the northern tip of Borneo, Sabah lies just clear of the belt of cyclones that regularly sweeps down across the Philippines and so has been dubbed by generations of sailors 'Land Below the Winds'. The coastal plain is inhabited by Bajau 'sea gypsies', most of them peaceful

Villages on stilts, such as this one in Kota Kinabalu, pepper the coast of Sabah.

fishermen, though a few still follow the centuries-old tradition of piracy. The inland hill-country is principally the home of Kadazan rice and vegetable farmers.

The Crocker Range, rising in Sarawak, culminates in Sabah in Mount Kinabalu. The mountain is the focus of a superb national park, just as the state capital, Kota Kinabalu, serves as a landing-stage for visits to an offshore national park of coral islands. On the east coast, Sandakan provides a base for visiting the Turtle Islands and the famous orang-utans of Sepilok.

Kota Kinabalu

Known as Jesselton until World War II, it was all too aptly renamed Api ('fire') by Japanese occupying troops, until Australian forces burned it to the ground to deprive the enemy of a strategic base. Rebuilt in a rather non-descript modern style, it is at least blessed with a beautiful natural setting: tree-clad coral islands off the coast and the dramatic backdrop of the mountain to the west. It is from the mountain that the town takes its present name, usually short-ened to KK. For the visitor, the real assets are its good hotel resorts to use as bases for visiting the surrounding national parks.

The large golden-domed **State Mosque** at the corner of Jalan Tunku Abdul Rahman and Jalan Penem-pang is a rather showy example of the official religion's self-assertion in a state where Malay Muslims are in the minority. Up on a hill opposite the mosque, **Sabah Museum** is a pleasant modern stylization of the longhouse. It offers an attract-ive display of the folklore of the Bajau, Kadazan and upcountry Murut peoples—ceramics, bam-booware and weaving.

On the north side of town is Kota Kinabalu's proudest skyscraper, the gleaming **Sabah Foundation**, a 30-storey cylinder mounted on a polygonal pedestal to look like a flat-topped space rocket. Devoted to state educational projects, it has a revolv-ing rooftop restaurant (inquire about opening times) promising great views of the surrounding seas and mountains.

At the southern end of town, the white sands of **Tanjung Aru Beach** provide the town's most popular recreation facility.

The Coral Islands

Boats from the jetty at the Tanjung Aru resort hotel or on the waterfront opposite the downtown Hyatt Hotel take you out to the islands of the **Tunku Abdul Rahman National Park**. The beaches are first class for swimming and snorkelling and there are boardwalk trails into the islands' jungle interior. Bordering some of the islands opposite Kota Kinabalu are villages built on stilts to house Malay and Filipino fisher-folk. Even if you are not a snorkeller, it is well worth taking an island-hopping cruise, at sunset or very early in the morning.

Pulau Gaya is the largest of the coral islands. The national park headquarters here can give you in-formation about the flora and fauna, both underwater and in the forest. The sandy **Police Beach** on the north shore is fine for swimming and exploring marine life among the coral reefs. On the boardwalk trail across mangrove swamp forest, look out for monkeys, bearded pigs and giant-beaked pied hornbills.

You will find some of the best nature trails on neighbouring **Pulau Sapi**. The coral reef near the jetty is a favourite haunt of anemone fish and damsel fish. You may be

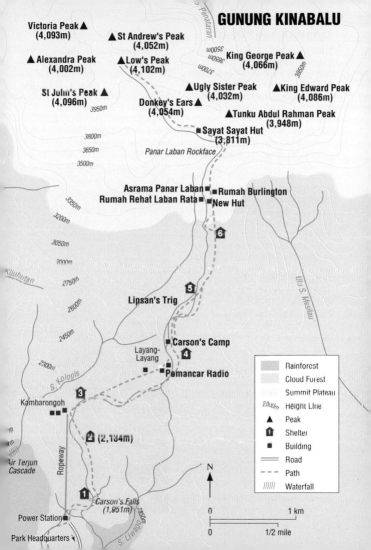

GUNUNG KINABALU

Victoria Peak ▲
(4,093m)

▲ St Andrew's Peak
(4,052m)

King George Peak ▲
(4,066m)

▲ Alexandra Peak
(4,002m)

▲ Low's Peak
(4,102m)

St John's Peak ▲
(4,096m)

▲ Ugly Sister Peak
(4,032m)

▲ King Edward Peak
(4,086m)

Donkey's Ears ▲
(4,054m)

▲ Tunku Abdul Rahman Peak
(3,948m)

■ Sayat Sayat Hut
(3,811m)

Panar Laban Rockface

3950m
3800m
3650m
3500m

Asrama Panar Laban ■
Rumah Rehat Laban Rata ■

■ Rumah Burlington
■ New Hut

6

3250m
3200m
3050m
3000m
2750m
2600m

Lipsan's Trig

5

■ Carson's Camp

4

Layang-Layang ■

■ Pemancar Radio

3

Kambarongoh ■■■

🏠 (2,134m)

1

Carson's Falls
(1,951m)

Power Station ■

Park Headquarters ↘

S. Penataran

3500m
3700m
3650m

Kiljuhutan

S. Koloris

Ropeway

S. Liwagu

Ulu S. Mesilau

Air Terjun
Cascade

N

	Rainforest
	Cloud Forest
	Summit Plateau
~~20km~~	Height Line
▲	Peak
🏠	Shelter
■	Building
——	Road
- - -	Path
)))))	Waterfall

0 _____ 1 km

0 _____ 1/2 mile

joined there by monkeys swimming out to fish for crabs. They are competing with white-bellied sea eagles. Chalets or camping and barbecue facilities are available. At night, you may see the scaly pangolin ant-eater that looks more reptile than mammal, rolling up into a ball when attacked.

South of Sapi, the coral off **Pulau Manukan** has been damaged by dynamite fishing and is only slowly recovering. Tiny **Pulau Mamutik** is unspoiled, with plenty of good coral at its north-eastern corner. The remotest island, with the park's finest coral reefs and abundant marine life, is **Pulau Sulang**. You can camp overnight here. (Remember that picking coral is forbidden.)

Around Kota Kinabalu

Make an excursion up the northern coast road to visit one of the many lively **village markets** (*tamu*) held on different days of the week—check on dates at Kota Kinabalu's tourist information office in the Sinsuran Complex (block L). Besides the usual fish, meat, fruit and vegetables brought in by Bajau and Kadazan farmers, you may also see auctions of horses and water buffaloes. The outfits of Bajau cowboys would put Hopalong Cassidy to shame. The best *tamu* are at **Tuaran** and further north at **Kota Belud**.

On your way to the village of Tuaran, make a side trip to the **Mengkabong water village**, built on stilts over a lagoon. The Bajau houses are linked by rickety boardwalks, but it is more usual to take a *sampan* canoe from one end of the village to the other. There is a handicraft shop for tourists.

Straddling a lagoon: the Mengkabong water village.

At the northern end of the coast road, **Kudat** boasts the state's most secluded beaches for people who really want to get away from it *all*.

The Beaufort Railway

Unlike the peninsula, East Malaysia never benefited from Britain's development of railways in the 19th century. But south of Kota Kinabalu, the Beaufort–Tenom jungle railway makes up in charm for what northern Borneo has lost in efficiency. Although the train begins at Tanjung Aru, you can save time for the most interesting stretch by taking a taxi to Beaufort and another from Tenom back to Kota Kinabalu.

At **Beaufort**, Chinese shop-houses stand on stilts beside the Padas River. The forest through which the train passes is the hunting-ground of Murut tribesmen, looking mainly for wild boar. At **Tenom**, they trade with the Chinese merchants in jungle medicines and edible birds' nests.

Mount Kinabalu National Park

The park is one of the best organized in the country, with experienced forest rangers giving you marvellous insights into the plant- and wildlife of the region. The journey from Kota Kinabalu to the park and climb up the mountain takes you through Malaysia's varieties of forest and landscape, from coastal mangrove to dipterocarp, cloud forest, montane and subalpine meadow.

At 4,100m (13,450ft), Kinabalu is the highest peak between the Himalayas and New Guinea. Its name means 'sacred home of the dead' to the Kadazan who dwell on its lower slopes. The park covers 754sq km (291sq miles) with temperatures much, much cooler than on the coast. They ease to a gentle 20°C (68°F) at park headquarters and drop to freezing point at the lodge where climbers spend the night prior to their

Gunung Kinabalu, the highest peak in Malaysia, is set amid the magnificent national park of the same name.

pre-dawn assault on the summit. So warmer clothing is a must for park visitors—and rainproof clothing, too, for those climbing the mountain. Unless you are an experienced climber, we once again recommend that you enlist the help of a tour guide.

In fact, the majority of visitors are quite happy just exploring the beautiful forests around park head-quarters. They get a clear view of the mountain's peak early in the morning, but by midday it is clothed in mists. Those who do go up the mountain each year number about 10% and are rewarded with a mag-nificent sunrise over Borneo—and a certificate to prove they did it.

The park is a 90km (56-mile) drive from Kota Kinabalu and offers a good restaurant and a wide range of accommodation, from individual chalets to simple hostels. There are informative slide shows, guided tours and maps of the trails for those who want to set out on their own (but be careful as some trails are not as well marked as others). Those of a hardy constitution may like to take a swim in the cool Liwago River nearby. A small but comprehensive **Mountain Garden** provides a good introduction to the plant life you will find in Kinabalu's forest.

Plant Life

The pride of the mountain is its 1,200 different orchids found up to an altitude of 3,800m (12,464ft). Ferns are also present in their hundreds.

Rhododendron-lovers will find 26 different varieties. But the most fas-cinating remain the pink-speckled carnivorous pitcher plants. Look out, too, for the bracket fungus, growing out of tree trunks to form a seat big and strong enough for a child to sit on. Other remarkable mushrooms here include the finger-like orange fairy clubs, white goat's-eyes, crim-son and pink sunburst fungi and buff-coloured phallus fungi.

Wildlife

Many of the local forest's 100 mam-mals are difficult to spot—the few orang-utans, for instance, are practi-cally invisible, but you can at least *hear* the gibbons whooping. Besides the usual sambar and mousedeer, bearded pig and clouded leopard, there are 28 species of squirrel. They range from the black giant squirrel, measuring up to 90cm (close to 3ft) from nose to tail-tip, weighing in at over 2kg (4.5lb) and the flying squirrel (who actually just jumps remarkably well) to the pygmy 8cm (3in) short.

Children adore the tiny wide-eyed doll-like slow loris—slow because that is how he moves—and the tarsier. The Kadazan describe the tarsier as some kind of com-pendium, with the 'tail of a rat, eyes of an owl, feet of a frog, ears of a bat, nose of a squirrel, fur of a loris and torso of a monkey'.

At night, the street lamps around the park HQ attract thousands of moths from the jungle. They make an ideal breakfast for the birds the next morning at dawn, when all self-respecting birdwatchers are up with their binoculars. Kinabalu has 250 species to offer, including the scarlet sunbird, long-beaked spider-hunter, fork-tailed grey drongo, crested serpent eagle, white-rumped shama and hysterical laughing thrushes.

But spare a thought, too, for the moths, notably the beautiful long-tailed 'Moon' moth and the giant 'Atlas', up to 25cm (10in) long.

Climbing Mount Kinabalu

The record for the climb is around three hours up *and* down, but ordinary mortals do it in two days. (Meals and bedding are provided at the mountain lodges for the overnight stop.) Armed with warm and rainproof clothing for the mountain mists, pocket torch, and a stock of bananas and chocolate for extra energy, you make an early morning start. After a stretch of road, the climb proper begins at **Timpohon Gate**. As you climb, you will notice the change from bamboo groves to oaks (the forest here has 40 different varieties), myrtle, laurel and moss-covered pines. The trees become progressively more gnarled and stunted as you approach the barren granite plateau at the summit.

The first shelter at **Carson's Falls** is at 1,951m (6,400ft). Your best chance to see pitcher plants on the trail is at the **Second Shelter** at 2,134m (7,000ft), but remember, no

picking. You make your overnight stop at the **Laban Rata Resthouse** or the **Panar Laban hostels** at 3,353m (11,000ft). *Panar Laban* means 'Place of Sacrifice', for it was here that seven white chickens and seven eggs were offered by Kadazan climbers to the spirits of the sacred mountain—and then eaten by the worshippers at a hearty banquet.

To get to the summit at sunrise, you must be up at 3 a.m. You make your way up across a barren plateau of flaked and pitted granite. The **Sayat Sayat huts** at 3,811m (12,500ft) are the last shelter before the summit. Immediately to the north are the **Donkey's Ears** rocks as you make your way west to **Low's Peak**, at 4,102m (13,455qqft) the highest of the mountain's nine peaks. (Colonial officer Hugh Low, a highly successful Resident in Perak, climbed the mountain in 1851.) Even if the altitude does not take your breath away, the view over the Crocker Range and out to the Philippine islands will. But you cannot loiter long on the summit to enjoy it, as it will soon be enveloped in midmorning mists, making the descent treacherous for even the most experienced climber.

Poring Springs

After a long trek, whether you have been up the mountain or not, your aching bones will welcome the soothing hot sulphur baths of this resort 43km (26 miles) east of the park HQ. Cool off at the **Langanan**

Waterfall, a site rich in butterflies and bat caves. *Poring* means bamboo and the surrounding bamboo forest is a delight in itself. It is one of the few places in the world where you may get a chance to see the giant **Rafflesia flower** (see p46).

Sandakan

After a short-lived boom busted by greedy clear-felling of the forest's hardwoods for the Japanese market, the town has returned to the more relaxed atmosphere of a fishing port. The seafood is among the best in Malaysia. But the town serves principally as a starting-point for trips to the wildlife sanctuary at Sepilok and the Turtle Islands north of Sandakan Bay. Closer to town, the beach at **Pulau Berhata** offers a relaxing swim when you get back from your excursions.

The Kinabatangan River

Tour operators at Sandakan organize three- or four-hour river-cruises to catch a glimpse of the elusive **proboscis monkey**. The Kinabatangan is a rewarding river for wildlife enthusiasts, as it also provides a rare opportunity to take a leisurely look at elephants, hairy-nosed otters and orang-utans in the wild.

☑ The Sepilok Orang-utan Sanctuary

A 30-minute drive west of Sandakan, the nature reserve provides a rehabilitation centre for orang-utan orphans, preparing them to return to the

forest and fend for themselves. Boardwalk trails and muddy paths take visitors through the forest to the feeding centres.

These highly theatrical russet-furred apes (see p50) exist at three levels in Sepilok's rainforest: tame, entirely in the care of zoologists; semi-tame, living within reach of the sanctuary's feeding points; and wild, having moved off to the remote parts of the forest away from their prying human cousins. Many of the orang-utans are as curious as the visitors. They have flashy tastes, preferring to snatch at bright objects rather than dull ones. They have a good sense of parody. Watching

Traders selling their wares in Sandakan, Sabah.

someone put up an umbrella in the rain, they will immediately mimic this, using leaves and twigs. And they show a weary disdain for the antics of photographers leaping around them.

The most optimistic figure for the total orang-utan population is 10,000 in Sabah and perhaps another 5,000 in Sarawak, but unbridled logging in their stomping grounds may have cut these numbers by half.

No large mammals share the Sepilok forest with them, but you may see giboons, pig-tailed macaques and red leaf-monkeys (not to be confused with the bigger tailless orang-utans).

The Turtle Islands

From June to September, green and hawksbill turtles gather to lay their eggs on the island beaches north of Sandakan Bay. Though the turtles also come to **Pulau Bakingan** and **Pulau Gulisan**, you will find chalets on **Pulau Selingan** from which to stage your overnight vigil. You can watch both egg-laying and the hatching of baby turtles, who then make for the safety of the sea (see p109).

SINGAPORE STOPOVER

If you intend to make a prolonged visit, you will find a more detailed account of this fascinating island republic in the BERLITZ TRAVEL GUIDE—SINGAPORE. Here, as many people fly into or out of Singapore on their Malaysia trip, notably for the duty-free shopping, we would just like to give you a few highlights for a short stay of one or two days.

The island, joined by a causeway to Johor Bahru at the southern tip of the Malaysian peninsula, covers 590sq km (228sq miles), roughly the size of metropolitan Chicago. An independent republic since 1965 (see p34), a third of the country is sprawling city dominated by skyscrapers. The rest is tailored hills and fields, with only occasional groves of lush green woodland to recall the time when all was jungle and swamp. The humid heat—30°C (86°F) by day, 23°C (73°F) at night—nurtures some of the world's finest orchids, but highly efficient air-conditioning makes life tolerable for mere humans.

Land is still being reclaimed from sea and coastal swamp for the construction of industrial estates. Singapore is Asia's largest oil-refining centre (third in the world), the world's fourth busiest port, and has one of the largest airports in the new Airtopolis. It is also a major focus for banking and stock trading, and sustains thriving machinery and sophisticated electronics industries. Its duty-free retail business in imported cameras, computers and jewellery makes it a paradise for consumers who think of Singapore City as one giant shopping mall (see pp152–3).

The causeway to Malaysia carries much of Singapore's food by road and rail as well as water by pipeline. But with this Islamic nation for a neighbour, the taste of Singapore's Chinese majority for pork has forced the island to become self-sufficient at least in pigs.

Three-quarters of the 2,650,000 population are Chinese, 15% Malays and 7% Indians. Even more tolerant than Malaysia, the island boasts some 500 Chinese and Hindu temples, Muslim mosques, Christian churches for its Eurasians and Westerners, and even a couple of Jewish synagogues. English, used without nationalist inhibition, is the *lingua franca* spoken between communities—in addition to their own Mandarin or Tamil and five Indian dialects.

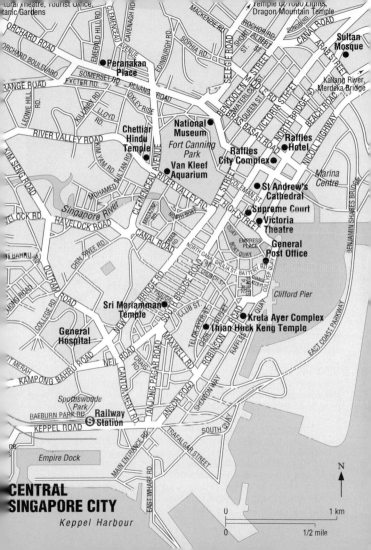

SINGAPORE CITY

Driving in the city centre requires special commercial or residential permits, so if you are not taking a guided tour, take a taxi, public bus or, for short trips, a trishaw. A good way to get a feel for the city is to ride upstairs the double-decker bus No. 140. This starts out from the Toa Payoh housing estate through the tourist hotel district on and around Orchard Road, along the waterfront to Prince Edward Road and back.

Chinatown

Sign of the age-old domination of Singapore by the Chinese, the heart of the old neighbourhood around South Bridge Road is known as 'Big Town' (*Tua Poh*). But, sign of the times too, it is shrinking every day as another block of old shophouses is swept away to make room for office skyscrapers. Still, a few groceries, apothecaries and street food-hawkers hang on. You can wander around stalls of live eels, gnarled

(Above) Skyscrapers are increasingly encroaching on Singapore's skyline. (Left) The more traditional side of Chinatown.

ginger root, decorated lanterns and freshly slaughtered python meat.

Chinese temples abound but the most famous shrine is **Sri Mariamman**, the oldest Hindu temple on the island, practically founded with Singapore itself in the early 19th century. Inside its South Indian *gopuram* tower profusely decorated with statues, you will find the temple's presiding goddess. She won allegiance for her cures for the smallpox and cholera that were prevalent when the colony was established. It stands next to the **Chulia Mosque**.

In **Sago Street** you will see elaborate paper models of cars, mansions and other material riches, burned by the Chinese after funerals to accompany the deceased into the hereafter. They are awaiting ceremonies organized in **Sago Lane** ('Death House Alley'). Here, modern undertakers have replaced the old death houses where dying Chinese awaited their end in hired rooms, surrounded by mourning friends and relatives. After dark, it is still the scene of flaming funeral ceremonies.

Among the remaining shophouses, look out for the few surviving makers of papier-mâché masks and wooden clogs, footwear that is still useful when the rains flood the streets. In **Club Street**, craftsmen carve highly-prized (and priced) gilt sandalwood statuettes of Buddhist and Taoist deities.

On colourful **Telok Ayer Street**, you will see Singapore's oldest and most important Hokkien Chinese temple. **Thian Hock Keng** (Temple of Heavenly Happiness) was built with granite pillars shipped over from the Hokkien district of southern China in 1840.

The Waterfront

Land reclamation on the downtown stretch of the Singapore River has moved the colourful junks, *sampan* river boats and *tongkang* lighters west to the wharves at Pasir Panjang Road. The **statue of Merlion**, half-fish, half-lion still guards the estuary, and lovers meet on the benches of Merlion Park. But it is the great **harbour** that now provides the waterfront's visual excitement. Beyond the park, the **Elizabeth Walk promenade** is a good spot from which to watch the action.

For a close-up view, take a harbour cruise in a motorized junk from **Clifford Pier** or the new passenger terminal at **Jardine Steps**. Your vessel coasts by freighters unloading cargo at the wharves and fights its way through countless scows, water-taxis, police-boats, tugs, schooners, yachts and the super-tankers that supply Singapore's half-dozen oil refineries.

Busy Clifford Pier stands at the end of **Change Alley**, a partly elevated shopping corridor where

---

Vestiges of the British Empire

*Few monuments remain from the British colony founded by Stamford Raffles in 1819. **Raffles' statue** stands on North Boat Quay on the spot where he is said to have first stepped ashore. On the same quay, **Parliament House** was built in 1827 as a private mansion, which later served as a courthouse.*

*Built in 1887, the **Raffles Hotel** on Beach Road, where Rudyard Kipling, Somerset Maugham and a lot of lesser writers quaffed their gin, has been re-furbished out of the price-bracket of all but the wealthiest scribes of today. But you may like to forgo half your duty-free purchases and eat at the renowned Tiffin Room or Grill Room.*

*With its central three-tiered steeple, the Catholic **Cathedral of the Good Shepherd** (1846) on Queen Street has a faint echo of Sir Christopher Wren to it. The Anglican **St Andrew's Cathedral** (1862) on Coleman Street is a nice Neo-Gothic. It was plastered beautifully white by masons from Madras who worked double-time when told the British would make human sacrifices to ward off evil spirits. Nearby on St Andrew's Street stand the 20th-century **City Hall** and **Supreme Court**, Singapore's last grand effort at Neo-Classical. It was at the City Hall that Lord Mountbatten accepted the Japanese surrender in 1945.*

money and goods change hands at lightning speed.

National Theatre District

On Tank Road opposite the National theatre is the **Chettiar Hindu Temple**, dedicated to the six-headed god Lord Subramaniam. It is richly endowed by the neighbourhood's money-lenders (*chettiar*). Ask a priest to show you, in an alcove to the right of the entrance, a cobra of pure hammered gold entwined around a bejewelled peacock.

Next door to the National Theatre, the **Van Kleef Aquarium** proposes a collection of some 4,000 specimens. The grey nurse shark plays host to turtles riding on its back. Less friendly are the crocodiles, Sudanese piranhas and electric eels. Many of the tropical fish have fanciful names: painted sweetlips and clown sweetlips, banded nandid and the beautiful yellow, black and silver poor man's moorish idol.

On Stamford Road across from the theatre, the venerable **National Museum** offers a splendid array of predominantly Chinese culture— Sung, Yuan and Ming porcelain, a rich collection of jade, rosewood and mother-of-pearl inlaid furniture, gongs, drums and silverware. But due attention is given to Malaysian and Indonesian arts and a documentation of the life of Sir Stamford Raffles. An interesting series of three-dimensional dioramas presents the history of Singapore from its earliest days as an ancient aboriginal settlement to its days as a British trading port under Japanese Occupation and the post-war campaign for independence.

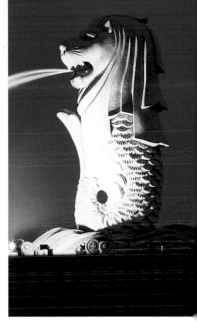

Singapore's Merlion guards the estuary.

Around Arab Street

Singapore's Muslims are a rich mixture of Malays and Indians who intermarried with 19th century Arab traders. Their neighbourhood has much of the atmosphere of a Middle Eastern bazaar, with aromas and

145

perfumes very different from those of Chinatown. Shops selling silks, Indonesian batiks, basketware and jewellery nestle around the minarets and domes of the **Sultan Mosque** in North Bridge Road near Arab Street. In the cool, carpeted interior of Singapore's largest mosque, the clock gives the time of Mecca. North Bridge Road also has some of the town's best Indian restaurants.

Up Arab Street across Canal Road's waterway, you plunge into the maze of stalls on Sungei, Kelantan and Larut roads known as **Thieves' Market**, open only in the afternoon. Hardware and antiques, both stolen and acquired honestly, are its speciality, but you will also find jewellery and fake designer clothes. If you are not careful, you may find yourself being offered a vaguely familiar watch, your own, purloined by the best pickpockets in the business.

The Gardens

To compensate for the relentless urban and industrial construction, Singapore has covered its island with parks and gardens. On Holland Road, the **Botanic Gardens**, founded in 1859, were a nursery for the Brazilian seedlings that launched Malaysia's rubber industry (see p28). Two ageing trees bear witness to this historic event. More aesthetically pleasing is the superb collection of orchids. Look out, too, for the fine collection of palms, the cannonball tree, sausage tree and the swans on a lily-covered lake.

Jurong Park on Yuan Ching Road offers an exquisite juxtaposition of Japanese and Chinese garden design. The tranquil **Japanese Gardens** (*Seiwaen*) present a harmonious landscaping of rock gardens, bridges and carp pools. The more extrovert **Chinese Gardens** (*Yu Hwa Yuan*) are inspired by the Peking Summer Palace. Climb the six-tiered Cloud-Piercing Pagoda and look out over the red and yellow pavilions, the Moon-Receiving Tower, the Fragrance-Filled Lily Pond and Jade-Splashed Bridge.

After this, **Tiger Balm Gardens**, 10km (6.5 miles) west of Singapore City on Pasir Pajang Road, come as a dreadful exercise in garish vulgarity, a Chinese theme park that children absolutely adore.

WHAT TO DO

Sightseeing is, of course, only a part of your visit to Malaysia. You will probably want to take time off to shop around for a piece of local handicraft, check out the night markets of Kuala Lumpur or Penang, or make a side-trip to the discount marts of Singapore. The country's sports facilities give you plenty of opportunities to unwind, not only at the beach. Or else you can just sit back and enjoy some of the traditional shows and festivities of a country that takes its leisure at least as seriously as its work.

SHOPPING

There has been a revival in traditional craftsmanship on the East Coast and Borneo. If you are hoping to find bargain-price electronic equipment and modern jewellery, your best bet will be a side-trip to Singapore. But there is no need to look further than Kuala Lumpur and Penang for masterfully faked watches and designer jeans. This is the Orient, so bargaining is part of the etiquette of shopping—except in government-run handicraft shops.

Batik, the colourfully patterned fabrics, are a popular buy.

147

WHAT TO DO

Craftwork

Most of the country's major towns have **handicraft shops** like Kuala Lumpur's Karyaneka Handicraft Centre on Jalan Rajah Chulan, that act as a showcase for products from all over the peninsula and East Malaysia. KL's Central Market gives you a wider selection. As far as quality is concerned, some of the best traditional products are to be found in the **museum shops** in Kuala Lumpur, Melaka, Kuching and Kota Kinabalu. The selection is more comprehensive in the markets and shops of Kelantan, Terengganu, Sarawak and Sabah. While in Kota Bharu or Kuala Terengganu, take a guided *kampong* tour to see the craftsmen at work—you'll often find you'll get their products at a better price than in town.

Batik

The gay, colourfully patterned fabrics are today both hand- and factory-made in Kelantan and Terengganu, but have their origin in the Malay kingdoms of Java over 1,000 years ago. The technique remains the same, although it was adopted in the peninsula only in the 20th century. A design of melted wax is applied to cotton or silk using a metal stencil. The fabric is then dipped in cool vegetable or synthetic dye which colours the cloth all around the wax pattern. It is then dipped in hot water to remove the wax. The process may be repeated for multiple colouring. Traditionally, certain designs were reserved for royalty, but today elegant geometric or exuberant stylized floral patterns are available to all. You can either buy the cloth and have it tailored back home or buy a sarong—useful at the beach over a bikini—a skirt, a shirt, a bag, a table cloth or a wall-hanging.

Kain Songket

Kain Songket (silk brocade) is a speciality of Terengganu. On a hardwood frame, silver and gold threads are woven into fine silk, usually of emerald green, dark red, purple or royal blue. Besides the geometric and floral patterns, you will also find handsome fan and dagger motifs. *Songket* was originally reserved for royalty, but is today also used for bridal dresses, other ceremonial robes, cushion-covers and handbags.

Silverwork and Pewter

The silversmiths' centuries-old skills, originally developed at the court of Perak, are continued today in rural Kelantan. Islam prohibits the representation of human or animal figures. This has the happy result of imposing much simpler patterns than the often excessively elaborate silverware across the border in Thailand. Besides ear-rings, brooches, necklaces and bracelets, you will find exquisite perfume

A Chinese artist in Kuala Lumpur.

bottles, snuff boxes (originally designed for betel nuts but useful for your anti-malaria pills or tranquillizers), belt buckles, caskets, lacquered trays and magnificent rice bowls.

Selangor Pewter, in the form of tankards, wine carafes, trays, salt- and pepper-pots, is a luxury side-product of the tin industry. It is actually 97% tin, hardened in a 3% alloy of antimony and copper. The best selection is at the factory on Jalan Pahang on KL's northern outskirts, but it is found in shops all over the country. It is also made and sold in Singapore, but at about the same price.

Other Craftwork

One of the most attractive products of the traditional arts is the highly decorative **puppet** used in *wayang kulit* shadow-theatre (see p154–5). The demons, clowns and kings that you can watch being made in a Kelantan rural workshop turn into splendid ornaments.

More practical but quite decorative are bamboo and rattan **baskets** and **mats** woven from nipa palm leaves. **Wood-carving** is another venerable Malay craft developed for the ornate door frames, beams and panelling of wooden palaces. But due to Islamic restriction on figurative representation, the **statuary** you will see is mainly aboriginal and for the most part rudimentary.

The **beadwork** of Sarawak and Sabah is very pretty—most often necklaces and bracelets, but also handbags and pillow cases.

In the Sarawak longhouses, you may be tempted to buy an authentic

---

Straight and Narrow Blowpipe

Kayan, Kenyah and nomadic Punan hunters make the best blowpipes (sumpitan) from coveted Sarawak straight-grained hardwood. From the felled tree, they cut a piece about 2.5m (8ft) long and shave it with an adze to a roughly cylindrical form about 10cm (4in) in diameter. This straight but rough pole is lashed firmly to a series of supports so as to stand perfectly upright. Its upper end projects above a platform where a craftsman—with a chisel-pointed iron rod as his drill—slowly, meticulously bores a dead straight hole down through the pole. The weapon's bore must be as clean and polished as that of a rifle barrel for the poisoned dart to pass through unimpeded. Its shaft is shaved, rounded and smoothed to produce a finished blowpipe of about 2.5cm (1in) in diameter.

The pipe oftens comes with a sharp spear point at its non-blowing end to finish off larger prey such as deer, wild pig—or, in the old days, you and me, who would only be stunned by the amount of poison on the tip of the dart. The poison is made from the sap of the ipoh tree.

---

blowpipe, one of the most accomplished pieces of indigenous workmanship in all Malaysia. Really good ones are increasingly rare and quite expensive, and their length, 2m (over 6ft), makes them hard to carry around. (Although no one is likely to try hijacking a plane with a blowpipe, it is better not to take it through airport security controls as hand luggage.) Failing a real hardwood blowpipe, you can buy the handsome quiver of stout rattan-bound bamboo with the poison darts (minus the poison), both authentic, and a shorter pipe of bamboo that does a perfectly serviceable job of blowing the darts into your cork dartboard.

Antiques

Melaka's Baba Nyonya Chinese quarter (see pp82–4) is a great place to hunt and bargain for old porcelain imported from southern China, antique silver or jade bracelets and, if you can find a way of shipping it home, a piece of furniture from the colonial days. In Penang, you may also occasionally hit on treasures—notably old Chinese theatrical costumes and splendid fake jewellery—as you rummage among the piles of junk in Georgetown's famous Rope Walk market.

Discount and Duty-Free Goods

The place to get a bargain on computers, tape-recorders, video and other electronic equipment is Singapore rather than Malaysia.

Computer buffs say that while Malaysia cannot compete with Singapore on 'hardware' prices, the deals on **computer software**, pirated or otherwise, are better in KL, Penang and Johor Bahru. If you cannot be bothered looking for discounts, you will find several good-quality **modern shopping centres** in KL on and around Jalan Bukit Bintang, near the bigger tourist hotels.

But you can get good deals in **watches**, **jewellery**, major brand **sports clothes** and **jeans** in the **street markets** of Kuala Lumpur—especially around Chinatown's Jalan Petaling—and of Georgetown along Jalan Penang, Lebuh Campbell and Lebuh Chulia. Bargaining is not just recommended here, it is almost compulsory. The fakes are best distinguished from the genuine articles by how low a price you can get. If you find you are acquiring an incredible bargain, start asking yourself whether that is what you want to pay for an albeit brilliant piece of counterfeit.

If all you are after is alcohol and cigarettes, the resort island of Langkawi has a duty-free concession.

Singapore

The discount shopping centres here rival those of Hong Kong without subjecting you to the latter's aggressive style of salesmanship. Notice that, except at the airport, no 'tax-free' or 'duty-free' signs are al-

A shopper's paradise: Jalan Petaling in Kuala Lumpur.

lowed in Singapore, since that advantage applies all over the island.

Those for whom shopping for a bargain is the main reason for going to Singapore should make some simple advance preparations:

1. Pack an extra fold-away bag to make room for bulky goods on the return trip.

2. If you are hunting for a well-known brand of watch, camera or piece of electronic equipment, go first to a dealer at home and note the exact model you want and the best price you can get there.

3. If you are after high-priced electronics equipment and do not want to risk the many counterfeit products on the market, call the manufacturer's local representative in Singapore to find out its authorized dealers. Even if their prices are not quite as low as those of their 'free-lance' competitors, they are still likely to be better than back home and you can sleep more soundly with the assurance of genuine equipment and proper international guarantees.

4. People looking for a new laptop computer to replace their old one should take along their software-diskettes for the Singapore dealer to transfer to the new machine. This is readily done free of charge, in the interest of the sale.

5. Give yourself plenty of time to shop around, so that you can compare prices. Knowing what the competition is like will give you more self-confidence when it comes to the expected practice of bargaining.

Everyone has his or her own technique for getting the best price, but a couple of general rules apply: decide in advance your spending limit and stick to it; and do it with a smile—these people have seen it all and will not be brow-beaten.

Best Buys

For **electronic equipment**, **watches**, and **cameras,** the major shopping centres are on Orchard, Tanglin, River Valley and Penang Roads.

Computers are best found at the Funan Centre on the North Bridge Road. But you should also look out for the following:

Antiques, including Chinese jade, ceramics, bronzes, gowns, incense burners and perfume bottles; Thai ceramics and bronzes; Indian brass; Indonesian wooden masks and carvings.

Carpets of both antique and modern design from China, Iran, India and Singapore itself.

Jewellery of jade, gold and silver at South Bridge Road and People's Park shopping centre.

Orchids in mixed sprays, which can be boxed and air-freighted abroad or carried with you.

ENTERTAINMENT

To cater to Western tastes, the major cities—KL, Georgetown, Melaka, Johor Bahru, Kuantan, Kuching and Kota Kinabalu—and the beach resorts have **nightclubs** and **cocktail lounges** with live music. The jazz and popular music scene is dominated by Filipino performers of very high quality. The singers deliver stunning carbon-copy renderings of current and past hit parades while the musicians are quite brilliant in their set pieces or improvisations.

Traditional Dance and Theatre

Malaysia's traditional entertainment is more often a daytime affair. Tourist information offices in Kota Bharu and Kota Terengganu can tell you about times and reservations for afternoon theatre and dance performances. These can also be seen at the Malaysian Tourist Information Centre in KL.

Mak Yong Dance Drama

This elegant art form evolved over some 400 years in the Malay state of Patani that is now part of southern Thailand, and is now performed across the border in Kelantan. It consists of a play on one of a dozen set romantic themes, accompanied by dance, operatic singing and knockabout comic routines. The latter is the preserve of the men while all the other performers are beautifully costumed women. The orchestra of bowed flute (*rebab*), gongs (*tawak-*

tawk), and double-headed drums (*gunang*) plays music with a distinctly Middle Eastern flavour.

Wayang Kulit Shadow Theatre

The most popular form of shadow theatre is known as *Wayang Siam*. It does not come, however, from Siam, as Thailand was once known, but is of Malay origin, drawing on themes from the Hindu epic *Ramayana*. It dates back over 1,000 years to when Indian merchants first brought their Hindu culture to the peninsula. The stories surrounding Prince Rama and his wife Sita

154

A lion dance troupe performs during Chinese New Year festivities.

involve ogres, demon-kings and monkey warriors, all represented on stage by puppets. With its customary cheerfulness, Malay culture has added a comic element absent from the high drama of the original.

The small timber and bamboo theatre is mounted on stilts and the puppets are seen as sharply etched shadows cast on a white cotton screen by a lamp hanging from the roof of the theatre. One puppeteer (*dalang*), accompanied by a band of musicians —playing the oboe, drums, gongs and cymbals—acts out all the parts and produces all the different voices, He peeps from behind the screen to assess the age and sophistication of his audience and varies the play accordingly. Originally, all the brightly coloured puppets were made from cow, buffalo or goat hides, but today the minor characters are turned out in plastic and celluloid. The bright colours are said to vary the intensity of the shadows and help differentiate the characters.

FESTIVALS

Malaysians love celebrating and with so many different religions—Islam, Hinduism, Buddhism, Christianity and aboriginal animism—they give themselves plenty of opportunities. They often join in each other's festivities, Muslims inviting Chinese friends to their Hari Raya feasts to end the fast of Ramadan, members of all the communities turning up for Melaka's Christian processions at Easter.

It is difficult to fix precisely the dates of the various festivals as most of them are fixed by lunar calendars which vary from year to year. This month-by-month listing can therefore only be approximate.

January/February: *New Year's Day*—1 January is a national public holiday.

Chinese New Year begins with a family dinner, and explodes with red banners and lion-dragon dances in the streets of Chinatown. (The noisy celebrations are meant to ward off evil spirits.) People wish each other *'Kong hee fatt choy'* (a happy and prosperous New Year) and exchange gifts including *ang pow*, red packets of money. Traditionally the festivities end on the 15th day, *Chap Goh Meh*, but the chamber of commerce usually likes to extend this highly profitable season by a week or two.

Thaipusam is the Hindu festival for Lord Murugan, celebrated with a procession of penitents seeking absolution at his shrine. The biggest is from KL to the Batu Caves (see p60).

March/April: *Easter*—peninsular Eurasians and indigenous Christian converts in Sarawak and Sabah celebrate with *Good Friday* processions, the most famous being organized by the Portuguese community of Melaka at St Peter's Church.

Ramadan—the great Muslim month of fasting is observed daily from sunrise to sunset, more strictly on the East Coast than the West. But everybody seems to like the festivities of *Hari Raya Puasa* ending the fast with three days of banquets.

Kelantan Kite Festival takes advantage of favourable winds to stage state-wide kite-flying contests (see pp161–2).

Hindu New Year (Chithirai Vishu) is a more religious affair than the Chinese, with worship and prayers.

May: *Sabah Rice Harvest Festival (Tadau Keamatan)* is celebrated by the Kadazan of Sabah with lots of rice wine and buffalo races.

Kota Belud Market Festival includes, among the local folklore, some spectacular high jinks by Bajau cowboys on horseback.

June: *Sarawak Rice Harvest Festival (Gawai)*—enlivened by the rice wine, the Iban stage cockfighting and blowpipe contests.

Dayak Day—Bidayuh and Iban get together for round after round of

palm toddy, rice wine and other jollitics.

Festa de San Pedoa (June 29)—boisterous Christian tribute to Peter, the patron saint of fishermen, in Melaka where Portuguese community has its fishing boats blessed.

July/August: *Hari Raya Haji*—Muslim families celebrate the return of pilgrims from their journey to Mecca.

Festival of Hungry Ghosts—Chinese honour ancestors with prayers, banquets and Chinese opera.

National Day (Hari Merdeka) on 31 August is a national public holiday.

September: *Kelantan Top-Spinning Festival*—state contest for top top-spinners (see p162).

A milk jar being offered to Lord Murugan, during Thaipusam.

October/November: *Deepavali* Hindu Festival of Lights is the Indian community's major celebration, signalled by candles lit in the homes, family feasts and prayers in the temple.

Prophet Mohammed's Birthday is commemorated by processions and public readings from the Koran.

December: *Penang Carnival*—month-long merriment in the streets of Georgetown.

Christmas Day—celebrated throughout Malaysia as a national public holiday.

SPORTS

Malaysians enjoy their leisure time to the hilt and the facilities are correspondingly plentiful.

Water Sports

Most large hotels have their own **swimming** pools. The coolest and most exhilarating swim is to be had in the natural pools of the waterfalls of Taman Negara, Mount Kinabalu, national parks and forest reserves.

But if you prefer good sandy **beaches**, head for the East Coast. The beaches of Kelantan and Terengganu, especially the turtle beach of Rantau Abang, and further south at Johor's Desaru, haven't yet suffered too much from the industrialization polluting the West Coast. But Tioman Island has the best of the peninsula's beaches, particularly if you like secluded coves. On the West Coast itself, your

best bets are the resorts on Penang Pangkor or Langkawi islands. In Sarawak, the best beaches are northwest of Kuching, at Damai, Santubong or Bako National Park; in Sabah, either at Kota Kinabalu's offshore islands of the Tunku Abdul Rahman National Park or up at Kudah on the northernmost tip of Borneo; over on Sabah's east coast try the islands in and around Sandakan Bay.

The resorts offer excellent amenities for all types of water sports: **snorkelling**, **scuba diving**, **windsurfing**, **sailing** and **water-skiing**. Scuba divers should remember that the coral and other marine life are protected species and are not to be picked or damaged.

Travelling in a sampan in Terengganu.

Golf

The British have left their mark and the country has over 150 courses, with a choice of 9-, 18- and 27- hole. When the local course is private, as at the Royal Perak Golf Club at Ipoh, your hotel may be able to get you temporary membership if you are a *bona fide* member of a golf club back home. Take your card along.

The most 'comfortable' courses are in the cooler hill stations, notably Cameron Highlands and Fraser's Hill. The best of the courses is at Saujana Golf and Country Club near KL, but there are pleasant 18-hole courses on Langkawi island. Golfers say that the best resort course is the Bukit Jambul Golf Club in Penang.

Racket Games

The national sport is **badminton** and is played wherever a net, real or makeshift, can be set up for players to thwack the shuttlecock across to each other. Resort hotels provide proper courts.

Tennis facilities are also widely available but the climate makes it a sport best reserved for early morning or evenings when the courts are floodlit. Squash has become a popular racket game and facilities are widely available.

Fishing

Freshwater angling is a delight in the mountain streams of Taman Negara and Mount Kinabalu national parks or on Lakes Chini and Kenyir. Off the East Coast, try deep-sea fishing for barracuda or shark. In all cases, inquire first at tourist information offices about the necessary fishing-permits. (**Hunting** licences are so restricted that it is scarcely worth the trouble for the ordinary tourist.)

Traditional Malay Sports

Like the arts and crafts, ancient Malay sports and pastimes are practised almost exclusively on the East Coast, though you may also see demonstrations elsewhere at cultural centres in KL or Sarawak. The best time to see them is in the weeks following the rice harvest and during the special festivals that stage statewide contests (see pp156–7).

Kite Flying

Kelantan and Terengganu preserve a centuries-old tradition of flying ornamental kites measuring 2m (over 6ft) across and again from head to

The Cameron Highlands are a great place to practise your golf.

Horse racing in Kota Kinabalu.

tail. In *kampong* workshops you can watch fantastical birds and butterflies being made of paper (and increasingly nowadays of plastic, too) drawn over strong flexible bamboo frames. Village contests judge competitors on their most spectacular flying skills—height, dexterity and the musical humming sound produced by the wind through the kite-head. There are also tug-o'-wars in which contestants ensnare each other's kite and drag it across a dividing line.

Top-Spinning

Like kite flying, top-spinning is no mere kid's game. Adults can keep a top in motion for over 50 minutes. The top looks somewhat like a discus, made of hardwood with a steel knob of spike in the centre and a lead rim. Standard size is about 23cm (9in) in diameter. It takes some six weeks to complete what is considered to be a precision instrument.

Villages stage team games with the objective of keeping a top spinning for the longest time. Another derivative of the game, using a different kind of top, has for objective to knock the opponent's top out of the spinning area.

Sepak Takraw

This is a kind of volleyball played with a ball made of rattan which the players can hit with every part of their body except hands and forearms. A three-man team scores points each time the ball hits the ground on the opponent's court or if the ball is hit out of the court. One team has to head or kick the ball over the net to the other team, without contacting the ball more than three times in their side of the court.

Silat

This Malay martial art came from Sumatra some 400 years ago. It is performed with elegant stylized gestures either as a form of wrestling, or as fencing with a sword or a traditional *kris*, known as *pencak silat*.

EATING OUT

A meal in Malaysia can be as varied as the ethnic mix that makes up the country. Chinese, Indian, Indonesian and Thai recipes and ingredients all make their contribution to the culinary landscape. Malay cuisine itself is often a combination of these and something else.

WHERE AND WHEN TO EAT

In addition to the hotel restaurants, you will find conventional restaurants in the big cities, often perched on top of skyscrapers, offering panoramic views. Kuala Lumpur, Melaka, Ipoh and Penang's Georgetown all have high-quality Chinese, Indian and Malay restaurants, but few of them imposes the kind of formality Westerners may experience back home. Meal times are also less rigid, especially as the popular hawker's centres often serve all day long. Vegetarians need not worry: many Chinese and Indian shops sell only vegetarian food.

Food Stalls

The arena for a gastronomic adventure is the open-air hawker's centre of food stalls—or food court. The stalls line both sides of a street or surround a court filled with tables and each offers different dishes of seafood, meat, chicken or vegetables, barbecue, soup, noodles or rice. Every town has its popular venues: in

KL, Chinatown's Jalan Petaling; in Melaka, Glutton's Corner; in Penang, Gurney Drive; in Ipoh, Jalan Yau Tet Shin; in Kota Bharu, Jalan Padang Garong; in Kuching, at Lintang Batu.

Find yourself a free table, note its number and begin your round of the hawkers, placing your orders. You can watch your meal being cooked right in front of you, check how fresh the produce is and so on. But after a while the spectator-novelty will wear off and you will be happy to go back and sit at your table, nurse a beer and wait for the various dishes to be brought over to you. For a party of four, it is not uncommon for each person to end up eating a different national cuisine or a little bit of all of them.

Malay

Like the Indonesian cuisine with which it shares a common tradition, Malay cooking is rice-based, but the southern Chinese influence has also made noodles very popular. It benefits from an inventive use of coconut milk and the local spices, herbs and roots from the jungle.

The most common Malay dish is *satay*—pieces of chicken, beef or mutton (pork being forbidden, of course) skewered and cooked over charcoal. It is served in a spicy sauce of ground peanuts, peanut oil, chillis, garlic, onion, grated pineapple, sugar and tamarind water, with slices of cucumber and glutinous rice wrapped in palm leaves (*ketupat*).

Mee rebus is a combination of noodles with beef, chicken or prawns and soya bean curd cubes, in a piquant brown gravy. To say that *prawn sambal* is spicy would be an understatement. It is served with coconut milk with chillis and crushed lemon leaves.

Tahu bakar, a soya bean cake in a sweet spicy peanut sauce with cucumber slices, is served on a nest of bean sprouts. Rice seasoned with lemon grass, chillis, ginger and soya accompanies *beef rendang*, pieces of beef marinated in coconut milk.

Otak otak is a grilled banana-leaf 'packet' of fish paste with coconut.

For the unabashed sweet tooth, try *gula melaka* sago pudding with coconut milk and a syrup of palm sugar or the weird colour combination of *chendol*—coconut milk with red beans, green jelly and brown sugar.

Chinese

With the Chinese community so often dominant in the towns, you will often find more Chinese than Malay restaurants and food stalls. The cuisine has become universal and no longer needs an introduction, but adepts will be pleased to find in Malaysia such a wide range of regional dishes.

Local delicacies: freshly made doughnuts in Chow Kit and glutinous rice with fish curry (nasi dagang) in Terengganu.

Hokkien cooking specializes in noodles. Try *Hokkien fried mee*, moist noodles with prawn, squid, pork and vegetables. *Or chien* is a seasoned omelette with tiny oysters and spring onions. In Klang and KL, Hokkien chefs make excellent *bah kut teh*, a soup of pork ribs, garlic and herbs.

Eight-jewel chicken or duck, which is stewed and boned, is stuffed with diced pork, mushrooms, dried prawns, carrots and glutinous rice. *Carrot cake* is in fact more of an omelette made with a grated radish that the Chinese call 'white carrot'. Other Hokkien staples are *hay cho*, deep-fried balls of prawn, mashed pork and water chestnuts; *popiah*, a rice flour spring roll of shredded meant, turnip, bamboo shoot, bean sprouts, bean curd, prawn and garlic.

Teochew cooking is famous for its *steamboat*, a southern Chinese version of fondue—very big on KL's Jalan Petaling. Pieces of fish and seafood, meat, chicken and vegetables are dipped by each diner into hot stock in the bubbling 'steamboat' set in the centre of the table. At the end, the stock makes an excellent soup with which to finish the meal. Teochew cuisine is light and non-greasy, based principally on seafood.

165

> ### *Tropical Fruit*
> *Malaysia may not be able to match France's 400 cheeses, but it does have 40 different kinds of banana. The tiny ones are the sweetest while the big green ones are used for cooking. Connoisseurs sing the praises of the three-panelled rather than the commoner four-panelled banana. Most of the wild ones you will find in the jungle seem to be all seeds.*
>
> *Besides the common or garden watermelon and pineapple, there are some real exotica to be discovered. The largest of all is the huge pear-shaped **jack fruit**, hanging directly from the tree's trunk and main branches. The biggest measure nearly 1m (3ft) in length and have been known to weigh up to 40kg (90lb). Nicely tart in taste, the yellow flesh has a chewy consistency. Eating a whole jack fruit takes for ever.*
>
> *Without its hairy red skin, the white-fleshed **rambutan** is almost indistinguishable in taste from the lychee—delicious. The waxy yellow-skinned **starfruit** does not look like a star till you cut it in slices. It is refreshingly tangy.*
>
> *Once you get past the foul smell of **durian**, it really is very tasty. Addicts say 'Smell? What smell?' Spiky and big as a football, its flesh is rich and creamy, best of all in its wild state in the jungle.*
>
> *If you are a health nut, go for the vitamin-packed **guava**, green-skinned with white flesh, or **papaya**, green-skinned with orange pulp. Unhealthy thrill seekers find them both rather boring. Nothing to compare to the gorgeous, sensual **mango**, growing, it seems, in a dozen different varieties in every Malay's back garden.*

The fresh fish is sweet because it is first mixed with a very light mixture of sweet berry sauce, peanuts and sesame oil. *Or leon*, a Teochew dish, is boiled sweetened yam.

A favourite hawker stall noodle dish is *char kway teow*, with prawns, clams, bean sprouts and eggs fried in chilli and dark soya sauce. Ipoh claims to have the best bean sprouts and noodles on the peninsula, served with boiled chicken.

Hainan island has sent over many immigrants and with them the great dish, *Hainanese chicken rice*. The chicken is stuffed with ginger, boiled and served in pieces with onion-flavoured rice and a special sauce of pounded chillis, lime juice and garlick. Can it be bad? They also make a masterful *mutton soup* simmered with Chinese herbs, ginger and young bamboo shoots.

Nyonya

This aromatic and spicy cuisine is a blend of Chinese and Malay traditions developed by descendants of the Chinese who intermarried in the Straits Settlements, Melaka, Penang and Singapore. The result is a much spicier version of the many southern Chinese dishes mentioned above. Most famous in Penang is the *assam laksa* hot and sour fish-based noodle soup redolent of tamarind, lemon grass and curry spices.

Bubor cha cha is a coconut milk creation with pieces of yam, sweet potato, sago and coloured gelatine. The Nyonya version of *otak otak*, a fish cake wrapped in palm leaf with coconut milk, lemon grass and shallots is grilled.

Indian

The best Indian food stalls serve their curries, rice, fish, meat and vegetables, piled high not on a plate, but a broad expanse of banana leaf. Indians may be eating with their fingers, but you will be provided with a fork if you wish.

Most of Malaysia's Indian community comes from the south of the subcontinent, where the searingly hot curries are sweetened by coconut milk. North Indian restaurants use a lot of yoghurt and a more subtle variety of spices. Since World War II, their numbers have been increased by Muslim immigrants from Pakistan and Bangladesh, adding beef to the traditional mutton and chicken meat dishes. Many Hindu restaurants, particularly around the temples, are purely vegetarian, offering delicious variations on curried aubergines, tomatoes, potatoes, lentils and lady fingers, accompanied by traditional breads—*thusai, chapati, nand, roti canai* and of course *papadam*.

As universal now as Chinese food, the Indian and Indian-Muslim dishes you will come across include *biryani* rice and meat, fish or vegetables cooked all together, with nuts, dried fruit and spices; *tandoori* marinated pieces of chicken or fish baked in a clay oven, and *murtabah* rice-dough pancakes folded over chicken, beef or mutton, onion, eggs and vegetable. This is a handy take-away snack but is better eaten at the table dipped in curry gravy.

Drinks

With all those exotic tropical fruits just dropping off the trees, the best drink here is a simple fresh fruit juice— mango, lime, starfruit, watermelon, guava and pineapple being the most common. Malaysians like soya bean milk, often sold at markets in a balloon-like plastic bag with a straw. The cheapest local drink is coconut water, from green king coconuts, not from old hairy ones.

If you want local alcohol, try the potent rice wine in Sarawak and Sabah. *Tuak* is the first fermentation, *lankau* the second processing with yeast—a 'killer'.

The local beer is very, very good, but some prefer the brews imported from China, Australia, Japan, Germany and the US.

And the Singapore Sling? Only mad dogs and Englishmen would drink this World War I concoction of gin, cherry brandy, fresh lime juice, Cointreau or Benedictine and possibly bitters and soda. The real colonial's drink is still simply a *stengah*, whisky and soda with crushed ice, or *gin pahit*, gin and bitters. Cheers!

167

BERLITZ-INFO

CONTENTS

BLUEPRINT

A ACCOMMODATION

In Malaysia, accommodation ranges from five-star luxurious hotels run by international chains to the adequate *rumah tumpangan* (Malay for lodging house)—usually a shophouse converted into a hotel—and the really bare A-frame beach huts which offer comfort a notch above camping. The government regulates the industry by issuing licences to operate hotels and to sell alcohol, but there is no official rating system.

Hotels International-standard hotels can be found in the state capitals and popular holiday spots. They offer gleaming marble floors, thick-pile carpets, good service, discos, live entertainment, swimming pools, and restaurants serving Western, Chinese, Japanese and local food.

Two- or three-star hotels offer the basics, which ought to be comfortable enough: most have air-conditioning, and most are safe and decent.

Budget rooms Of late, budget rooms styled after the Bed and Breakfast concept have cropped up in Kuala Lumpur, Melaka and Penang. These are relatively clean, though you may have to use a common toilet. Lebuh Chulia in Georgetown is famed as a watering hole for backpackers.

Budget chalets Another recent development is the mushrooming of budget chalets along Malaysia's lovely beaches. These can be found in resort islands like Langkawi, Pangkor and Tioman, and along East Coast beaches like Cherating, Rantau Abang (where thousands turn up to watch giant leatherback turtles nesting from May till September) and Marang.

A bare room with bed, clean sheets, shower and toilet will cost as little as M$20 a night. For extra money, some will throw in a mosquito net—a necessity, as mosquitoes buzzing around your ears and making dive attacks on your body are not conducive to sound sleep. In the absence of a mosquito net, the trick is to burn a mosquito coil. These are green coils that look like incense sticks, but whose rather acrid smoke deters mosquitoes. Otherwise, turn the ceiling fan to maximum. If that doesn't work, your last resort is to find air-conditioned accommodation, which might be more expensive.

Rest houses These are bungalows formerly owned by English planters and civil servants, and now turned into holiday homes and hotels redolent of the British colonial past. You will find them at the hill resorts of Cameron Highlands and Fraser's Hill and in small towns. Most are privately owned.

Youth Hostels and YMCAs Malaysia may not have an extensive network of Youth Hostels and YMCAs, but the few available are adequate and clean. Hostels run by the Malaysian Youth Hostels Association can be found in Kuala Lumpur and Port Dickson. Other hostels affiliated to the association are in Melaka, Penang and Cameron Highlands. An overnight stay in a Youth Hostel costs about M$15. For bookings, call:

Kuala Lumpur: (03) 230-6870
Port Dickson: (06) 472-188
Melaka: (06) 515-778 (beach hostel) or (06) 235-124 (town hostel)
Cameron Highlands: (09) 941-145
Penang: (04) 630-558

YMCAs can be found in Kuala Lumpur, Georgetown and Ipoh:
Kuala Lumpur: 95 Jalan Padang Belia, tel. (03) 274-1439
Georgetown: 211 Jalan Macallister, tel. (04) 362-211
Ipoh: 211 Jalan Raja Musa Aziz, tel. (05) 540-809

The YMCA in KL offers the best value for money, with its non air-conditioned room for four at only M$40. A single air-conditioned room costs M$55, while a non air-conditioned room costs M$24.

CLASS	FACILITIES	PRICE
Luxurious (4–5 star)	Air-conditioned rooms, swimming pool, restaurants, coffee house, discos, business centres, bars, in-house video.	High (M$180–400)
Average	Air-conditioned rooms, coffee house, bar lounge, in-house video.	Moderate (M$90–150)
Economy	Rooms with ceiling fans, clean sheets and toilets.	Cheap (M$40–70)
	Beach chalet or A-frame hut with bed, clean sheets, shower, toilet/common.toilet.	Very cheap (M$20–30)

Please note that hotels of all classes are usually filled during local festivals (see PUBLIC HOLIDAYS) and school holidays. Students go on vacation for a week in January/February, a week in March, three weeks in June, a week in August and five weeks in November/December.

AIRPORTS

The major international airports are Subang near Kuala Lumpur, Bayan Lepas in Penang, Kuching in Sarawak and Kota Kinabalu in Sabah.

You can also fly into Malaysia via Pulau Langkawi, but the traffic is light. There are plans to build another international airport in Sepang, Selangor, to ease congestion in Subang. This is scheduled for completion in 1997. Another proposal is to have an international airport in Labuan, an island off Sabah and future International Offshore Financial Centre.

Subang Airport (Kuala Lumpur) 18km (11 miles) from the city; limousine taxi and regular bus service; duty-free shops; banks; currency exchange; car rental counters; tour booking counters; restaurants.

Bayan Lepas (Penang) 16km (10 miles) from Georgetown; taxis and buses to the city; duty-free shops; currency exchange; car rental counters; tour booking counters; restaurants.

Kuching (Sarawak) 10km (6 miles) from town; taxis and buses to town centre; souvenir shops; currency exchange; tour booking counters; coffee shop.

Kota Kinabalu (Sabah) 7km (4 miles) from town; taxi and buses to town centre; souvenir shops; currency exchange; tour booking counters; coffee shop.

Departure Tax
Domestic destinations: M$5
Singapore and Brunei: M$20
International destinations: M$20

ALCOHOL

There is no ban on alcohol in Malaysia. However, in certain States like Kelantan, Terengganu, Perlis and Kedah, there is stricter control on the sale of alcohol outside hotels because of the stronger Islamic influence in these predominantly Malay States. Only non-Muslims are allowed to purchase alcohol from shops and restaurants.

In KL and larger cities, supermarkets and stores stop selling alcohol at 9 p.m. Pubs and bars serve drinks until midnight.

When you visit a Sarawak longhouse, the Ibans (natives of Sarawak) will welcome you at every doorway with a glass of *tuak*, a sweet wine made from glutinous rice. It certainly is a warm way of breaking the ice. Sabah has its own version of the potent wine, which is called *tapai* over there.

CAMPING

There is no organized system for campers or those travelling by caravan in Malaysia. The few campsites available are reserved for Boy Scouts and Girl Guides. There are a few campsites in forest parks like Lake Chini, Taman Negara (the National Park) in Pahang and the Bukit Cahaya Seri Alam park in Shah Alam, Selangor, but you have to pay to be able to pitch your tent there. You can rent a two-man tent for M$6 per night and a four-man tent for double that amount. You also have to pay M$1 to register as a camper at Taman Negara. (It is not possible for caravans to get to Taman Negara.)

One company in Kuala Lumpur rents out motorhomes. A two-berth motorhome costs M$260 per day, while a four-berth van costs M$320. The motorhome comes with a full tank of petrol and the vehicle should be returned in the same state. International and foreign driving licences are accepted, provided that the driver is aged at least 25. You can drive the motorhome all over the country, stopping to rest wherever you like, as long as you don't have to feed a parking meter. A collision damage waiver costs M$10 per day. For reservations, call (03) 241-8541.

CAR HIRE

Several car rental companies, including some international names, are based in major cities. They can be found listed in the Yellow Pages. You will also find car hire counters at the following airports: Subang, Penang, Ipoh, Johor Bahru, Kuantan and Kerteh. Please note that it can be difficult to hire a car in Sarawak and Sabah.

Rates range from M$148–428 daily depending on the make and engine capacity of the car. A Proton Saga 1.3 can be hired at M$148 per day with unlimited mileage. A Mercedes Benz 200 will cost M$428 per day with unlimited mileage. Car hire companies accept only credit cards and there is a M$50 deposit for petrol.

You need an international driving licence or a valid licence from your own country. Drivers must be over 25 years of age.

CIGARETTES (*rokok*)

All leading brands of cigarettes are available in Malaysia. Some are imported while most are made locally. Cigarettes can be bought at sundry shops, coffee stalls, supermarkets, duty-free shops and newsagents. Major supermarkets stock French cigarettes and fine tobaccos too. Cigarettes are no longer as cheap as they used to be; the government has increased taxes as a measure to discourage smoking. A pack of 20 can cost from M$2–3.30.

CLIMATE

Malaysia is a tropical country and contrary to illusions created by travel brochures, the climate can be an irritant, especially if you have just departed from a country in the midst of winter. The Malaysian climate is hot, humid and wet. Daily lowland temperatures range from 21°C to 32°C (70°F to 90°F). Rainfall averages 250cm annually. Nights are generally cool, but afternoons are usually blazing hot; hence the saying that only mad dogs and Englishmen brave the noon sun in Malaysia.

Monsoons bring heavy rain. The north-east Monsoon lasts from November till February and the most affected areas are in the East Coast States of Kelantan, Terengganu and Pahang, and parts of Sabah. Due to adverse weather conditions, the National Park in Peninsular Malaysia is closed from the beginning of November to the middle of January. The south-west monsoon lasts from July till September. The rain is not as heavy because of the shielding effect of the Indonesian island of Sumatra.

It is not advisable to swim in the sea or travel in small boats off the East Coast during the north-east Monsoon. Other than that, the seas in Malaysia are generally safe for swimming, sailing and water sports.

CLOTHING

Since the climate is hot, humid and wet, you should wear thin, light-coloured and loose clothing, preferably made of cotton. At the hill resorts, a woollen sweater or vest would suffice.

Malaysians are a casual lot and even at fancy restaurants, you will find locals dressed in a relaxed manner. At a formal dinner or reception, a suit and tie or a long-sleeved batik shirt will do (this garment will get you into any respectable establishment in Malaysia, including the casino in Genting Highlands). However, sandals and slippers are considered too casual for restaurants and discos.

At the beach, anything goes except for topless or nude sunbathing.

For walking around, wear a pair of rubber-soled leather shoes (as leather breathes better and soles made of rubber has good shock absorption qualities) or good canvas walking boots, and wear cotton or woollen socks (since you are bound to sweat). Remember to take off your shoes before entering a place of worship or before entering a house. Malaysians usually take off their shoes before entering their homes.

If you happen to have large feet, buy your shoes before you leave home. Asian feet are smaller and large shoes beyond size 9 or 10 are difficult to find in Malaysia, where most men wear size 6–7 shoes. And if you intend to do some shopping in Malaysia, bear in mind that the Asian physique is also smaller. Shops stock mainly petite sizes. **Note** Refrain from wearing shorts or short skirts when visiting mosques and rural areas especially in the east coast states.

COMMUNICATIONS (see also HOURS)

Post Office The General Post Office in Kuala Lumpur opens from 8 a.m. till 6 p.m., Monday to Saturday. On Sundays, the GPOs in KL, Penang, Johor Bahru, Ipoh, Kuantan, Melaka, Kuching and Kota Kinabalu open from 10 a.m. to 1 p.m. Post offices in other towns open from 8 a.m. till 5 p.m. from Mondays to Saturdays, except in Kelantan, Kedah, Perlis and Terengganu where they close on Fridays and remain open on Sundays. Stamps are only sold at post offices but letters can be dropped into red post boxes found all over the place. Major hotels will also post your letters for you.

Malaysia has an express mail system called *Pos Laju*, which offers delivery within 24 hours to several countries around the world. This service is available only at major post offices.

Poste restante and telegram services are available at the main post offices of the state capitals.

Telephone Telephone cards are in use in Malaysia and some public phones can be used only with such cards. Coin-operated telephones are still around, but these are for local calls only. Out-of-state calls can be made by dialling area codes or with assistance from the operator.

International calls can be made at major hotels. At Jabatan Telekoms (Telecoms Department) offices in major cities and towns, overseas calls can be made and telexes sent.

International direct dialling, home country direct service, telefax, telegram and telex services are available at Telekoms outlets in Subang airport. Home country direct service is also available at the KL railway station.

Five star hotels have Business Centres where you can also fax documents overseas.

International calls:	108	**Trunk calls**:	101
Directory enquiry:	103	**Telegrams**.	104

CRIME AND THEFT

Malaysia is generally safe but, as in any other country, some basic rules apply.

- Don't accept drinks from strangers.

- Don't carry too much money in your wallet.
- Don't flaunt expensive jewellery in seedy places.
- Don't leave your bags or cameras lying around unattended.
- When visiting crowded places, beware of pickpockets.
- Dress in a sensible manner.

CUSTOMS AND ENTRY REGULATIONS

To enter Malaysia, you need a valid passport or visa. A disembarkation card has to be filled out and handed to Immigration officials on arrival. It is important to note that even though Sabah and Sarawak are in the federation of Malaysia, you need a passport to visit these East Malaysian States.

Visa requirements Holders of full British passports, Republic of Ireland passports and citizens of Commonwealth countries do not need a visa. Holders of US passports can enter Malaysia for three months without a visa.

Export of antiques and historical objects is not allowed unless an export licence is obtained from the Director General of Museums Malaysia or if the antique was originally imported and declared to Customs.

Foreign tourists have to declare to Customs or the plant quarantine inspector any flowers, plants, fruits or seeds, soil samples, cultures of fungi, bacteria or viruses, insects or any other vertebrate or invertebrate animals in their possession, and if they have visited any country in Tropical America or the Caribbean during the previous 30 days.

Visitors entering Malaysia for more than 72 hours enjoy tax exemption on several items:

- Not more than 225g of tobacco or 200 cigarettes or 50 cigars.
- Not more than one litre of wine, spirits/malt liqueur.
- Not more than three items of clothing.
- Not more than M$75 worth of food.
- Not more than one pair of shoes.
- One portable electrical and/or battery-operated appliance for personal use.
- Not more than M$200 worth of souvenirs and gifts—unless the goods are bought in Labuan, in which case the limit is M$500.
- Not more than M$200 worth of cosmetics, perfumery and soap in open containers.

	Cigarettes		Cigars		Tobacco	Spirits		Wine
Malaysia	400	or	50	or	250g	3l	or	3l
Australia	250	or	200	or	250g	1.1l	or	1.1l
Canada	200	or	50	and	1kg	1.1l	or	1.1l
Eire	200	or	50	or	250g	1l	or	2l
N Zealand	200	or	50	or	250g	1.1l	and	4.5l
S Africa	400	and	50	and	250g	1l	and	2l
UK	200	or	50	or	250g	1l	and	2.
USA	200	and	100	and	*	1l	and	1l

* A reasonable quantity

Currency restrictions Malaysia has a liberal system of exchange control and funds can be transferred freely in and out of the country. Provided that the currencies are declared on arrival, **import** of local currency is unlimited, as is import of foreign currencies. **Export** of the local currency is allowed up to M$2 million in banknotes; exporting more than this will require a special permit. Export of foreign currencies is unlimited.

Warning The trafficking of illegal drugs is a serious offence in Malaysia and the penalty for such an offence is death.

DRIVING IN MALAYSIA   D
In Malaysia, driving is on the left—a legacy of the British colonials. Road signs have been changed to Malay, but you will get by if you pick up a few words:

Jalan	*Road*
Lorong/Pesiaran	*Lane*
Jalan behala	*One-way street*
Pusat Bandar	*City centre*
Utara/Selatan	*North/South*
Timor/Barat	*East/West*
Lebuhraya	*Highway*
Tol	*Toll*
Berhenti	*Stop*
Simpang	*Junction*
Awas	*Danger*

The Highway Code is of the universal type and distances and speed limits are in metric. There is no fixed speed limit; it ranges from 90–110km/h on highways and from 30–80km/h in urban areas and town limits (55–70mph and 20–50 mph). Spy cameras and radar guns are in use to nab speed freaks. To play safe, check the speed limit signs every now and then.

Accelerated growth combined with lack of planning mean that the road systems in Kuala Lumpur and major towns can be confusing. But after a while, you will find some sense in the confusion. Most roads are named, except for satellite towns like Petaling Jaya where numbers are used instead.

Roads are generally of good quality and the new North–South Highway, which will eventually link Singapore to Thailand, is of international standard, though you have to pay a toll to use it.

E ELECTRICITY

The voltage is 220 volts throughout Malaysia. Electricity is widely available except in remote places and some islands where generators are used.
Note You will find square or round three-pin plugs in different establishments, whilst some old hotels use two-pin plugs. A universal adaptor is handy.

EMBASSIES AND HIGH COMMISSIONS
(All are in Kuala Lumpur)

Australia	6 Jalan Yap Kwan Seng, tel. (03) 242-3122
Canada	7th Floor Plaza MBF, Jalan Ampang, tel. (03) 261-2000
Great Britain	185, Jalan Ampang, tel. (03) 248-2122
New Zealand	193 Jalan Tun Razak, tel. (03) 248-6422
USA	376 Jalan Tun Razak, tel. (03) 248-9011

EMERGENCIES
Dial **999** if you need to contact the police, fire brigade or hospital. Major hotels offer medical services for minor ailments.

Police	**Polis**
General Hospital	**Hospital Besar**
Clinic	**Klinik**
Emergency ward	**Wad Kecemasan**
Road accident	**Kemalangan**
Help	**Tolong**
Fire brigade	**Bomba**

GETTING TO MALAYSIA **G**

Flying is the most common means of getting to Malaysia. The privatized national airlines, Malaysia Airlines (more widely known as MAS), fly from numerous destinations around the world, as do many other airlines, so that flights to and from major cities are not a problem. However, if you have more specific requirements, we suggest that you get in touch with your national TDC (see TOURIST INFORMATION OFFICES) and/or with a reputable travel agent.

GUIDES AND INTERPRETERS

Professional guides normally work for tour companies that organize inbound tours; very few of them work independently. You may choose to discover Malaysia on your own—many do. However, tours or treks into the more remote parts of the country benefit from the assistance of a guide. Get in touch with your national TDC or with the TDC in Malaysia (see TOURIST INFORMATION OFFICES), who may be able to advise you on the most reputable tour guides. Since English is widely spoken, tourists from English-speaking countries should encounter few language barriers.

HEALTH AND MEDICAL CARE **H**

Most major hotels provide some medical service for minor ailments. Every town has a government hospital, and major towns and cities boast private clinics and hospitals. Doctors, nurses and other medical staff speak English, and chances are high that they will have obtained their qualifications from British universities.

Unless you're adventurous and have a lead-lined stomach, don't drink or eat at hawkers' stalls. Though the tap water is chlorinated, drink boiled or bottled water. Lay off curries and spicy foods unless you're used to such exotic fare.

Pharmacies, usually located in department stores, close at 9 p.m.

HEALTH REGULATIONS

- A valid vaccination certificate against smallpox is required from any traveller above six months of age who has visited a smallpox-infected country up to 14 days prior to arrival in Malaysia.

- A valid vaccination certificate against yellow fever is required from any traveller above one year of age who has visited a yellow fever in-fected country up to six days prior to arrival in Malaysia.

- If you plan to trek in the jungle, take anti-malaria pills. It is also advisable to have an anti-Hepatitis B jab.

HOURS

Malaysia has a dual system regarding the opening hours of government offices. In the States of Kelantan, Terengganu, Perlis, Kedah and Johor, the weekend is on Thursday and Friday. Thus government offices open during Saturdays and Sundays, close at 12.45 p.m. on Thursdays and are shut all day on Fridays.

On other days, government offices are open from 8 a.m. to 4.15 p.m. Banking hours are from 10 a.m. to 3 p.m.

In the States of Selangor, Perak, Negeri Sembilan, Pahang, Melaka, Penang, Sabah and Sarawak, government offices are open from 8 a.m. to 4.15 p.m. Mondays to Fridays and from 8 a.m. to 12.45 p.m. on Saturdays. Banking hours are from 10 a.m. to 3 p.m. Mondays to Fridays and from 9.30 a.m. to 11.30 a.m. on Saturdays. The lunch break is longer on Fridays because it's prayer time for Muslims.

Generally, the private sector throughout Malaysia follows normal hours. Companies open from 9 a.m. to 5 p.m. on weekdays and from 9 a.m. to 1 p.m. on Saturdays. Post offices are open from 8 a.m. to 5 p.m. (6 p.m. in KL's GPO) from Mondays to Saturdays, except in Kelantan, Kedah, Perlis and Terengganu, where they close on Fridays and open on Sundays. (See also COMMUNICATIONS.)

Shops open daily till 6–7 p.m. Major department stores open till 9.30 p.m. or 10 p.m. Museums close at 6 p.m.

L LANGUAGE

Bahasa Malaysia, or Malay, is the national language. Tamil is the main Indian dialect spoken in Malaysia, and Mandarin and many Chinese dialects are also practised. But English is widely spoken; there shouldn't be any communication problems unless you are in a remote area. Most signs are written in romanized Malay and you should be able to recognize the most common ones.

Shop	**Kedai**
Bus	**Bas**
Taxi	**Teksi**
Telephone	**Telefon**
Hotel	**Hotel /Rumah**
Lodging house	**Tumpangan**
Do you speak English?	**Bolehkah anda cakap Bahasa Inggeris?**

LOCAL TRANSPORT

No city in Malaysia has an underground train transport system. Cities and town are serviced by buses and in Kuala Lumpur, a complementary service is offered by minibuses. Taxis, mostly air-conditioned, are readily available and fares are metered, though in some places, like Penang, cabbies do not use the meter. This is mostly due to a lack of enforcement by the authorities. In such places, negotiate the fare before boarding. In the city, taxis can be found at main taxi ramps or flagged down anywhere.

In the East Coast towns of Kuala Terengganu and Kota Bharu, trishaws are a popular mode of transport. Some of them are gaudily decorated and make for good photographs. West Coast towns like Georgetown in Penang and Melaka also have trishaws. Trishaw rides to destinations within town limits shouldn't cost more than M$3, but it is advisable to agree on a price before setting off.

Intra-city travel is cheap and getting from one part of town to the other would not cost more than M80 cents. Minibuses in Kuala Lumpur charge a flat rate of M60 cents.

LOST PROPERTY

If you lose a bag in the airport, go to the Lost Baggage Department. If you lose something in the city, your best bet is to approach the police. If you leave something in a taxi, it is possible to trace the cabbie if he is driving a call-cab. Telephone the call-cab company and provide details of the item(s) left behind.

MAPS

M

The Tourist Development Corporation of Malaysia publishes maps of various places of interest in Malaysia. You can find these at hotels, Tourist Information Centres, major airports and train stations. More detailed maps can be bought at leading bookshops. However, the one problem Malaysia seems slow in solving is the absence of good road maps. This dates back to the paranoia created during the Emergency, when it was feared that detailed maps would fall into the hands of communist forces. The threat has disappeared but not, apparently, the old fears.

MEETING PEOPLE

Malaysians are very hospitable and friendly. Say hello and they will immediately return your greeting and possibly strike up a conversation. In certain popular areas like Tioman Island, Cherating Bay in Pahang, Marang in Terengganu and Langkawi Island, many villagers have converted their homes into budget chalets and staying in such places will enable you to experience to some degree the Malaysian way of life.

Some tour companies offer visits to Malaysian homes during festivals like the Chinese New Year and Hari Raya Aidil Fitri (a Muslim festival marking the end of the holy month of Ramadhan). Malaysians celebrate festivals by having open houses, where neighbours, friends and relatives can drop in and help themselves to goodies and drinks.

Some taboos Malays don't like pointing or being pointed at with fore-fingers; point with your thumb instead. They also feel it is not courteous to hand over or receive things with the left hand; make it a point to use your right hand even if you are left-handed.

MONEY MATTERS
The monetary system is metric. One hundred sen make one ringgit.

Coinage: 1, 5, 10, 20 and 50 sen. M$1 coins have just been minted and will soon replace banknotes.

Banknotes: M$1, M$5, M$10, M$20, M$5 , M$100, M$500 and M$1,000.

Keep 10-sen coins for local telephone calls. If you plan to make lots of calls, buy a telephone card. Vending machines for canned drinks and coffee accept 10, 20 and 50 sen coins; some accept M$1 notes as well as M$1 coins. Parking meters accept 10, 20 and 50-sen coins.

Banks & currency exchange Traveller's cheques are accepted at all banks. Popular credit cards can be used at major hotels, department stores and some shops. Currency can be exchanged at banks or licensed moneychangers which operate beyond banking hours. Most licensed moneychangers close at 8 p.m. Exchange rates differ from bank to bank, so shop around for the best deals.

N NEWSPAPERS
Malaysian newspapers are a reflection of the multi-racial society. Thus there are English, Mandarin, Malay (in romanized Malay and *Jawi*, an Arabic script) and Tamil newspapers and magazines published by local companies. Local English-language newspapers are *New Straits Times*, *The Malay Mail*, *The Star and The Sun*. They are available at all news stands.

Newsagents in leading hotels and major bookshops sell foreign news-papers at relatively high prices. On top of that, the foreign newspapers arrive very, very late. Magazines covering news, sports, hobbies, fashion, etc. are widely available.

NIGHTLIFE
Malaysia's nightlife is bustling, and this is especially so in Kuala Lumpur, Petaling Jaya, Penang, Johor Bahru, Kota Bharu, Kuching, Melaka and Kuantan.

Discos and pubs are popular watering holes for nightbirds. Five-star hotels normally have discos where the parties do not end till 2 a.m. on weekdays and 3 a.m. on Saturdays. Kuala Lumpur has the largest number of nightspots and one road there, Jalan Pinang, boasts a row of discos.

And if you do not like bars and discos, there are enough food stalls and night markets for you to explore. Night markets are colourful places which should not be missed. These open-air markets trade from 6 p.m. to 10 p.m. (The most famous night market is at Jalan Petaling in KL.)

PHOTOGRAPHY P
Malaysia is a photographer's paradise. From the beauty of nature deep in the jungle to white sands washed by clear seas, Malaysia offers sights that you will want to record on film.

Films and processing are relatively cheap. Processing quality has improved and shops displaying the Fotoplus sign have their equipment and chemicals checked regularly by Komal (Kodak Malaysia). Fuji is also taking steps to ensure high processing standards.

Most shops stock colour negative films. Slide films can be found only in leading photography shops in major towns. So stock up on slide films before moving around the country. Take note that not many shops sell Kodachromes or black and white film.

The sunlight in Malaysia can be harsh and the best periods to take pictures are in the mornings and evenings. Furthermore, be careful with your exposure readings. Overexposure is a frequent occurrence.

In Malaysia, you can photograph anything except some Malay women in the East Coast who are quite shy. If you can, avoid taking photographs of Muslims in prayer in mosques. It is forbidden to take photographs in museums and art galleries.

POLICE
Policemen wear grayish-blue shirts and khaki trousers while their female counterparts wear grayish-blue dresses.

Police stations can be found in almost every city and town in Malaysia. Cities like Kuala Lumpur and Georgetown have police districts, but reports can be lodged at any station.

Police	**Polis**
Police station	**Stesyen Polis**
Report	**Lapuran**

PUBLIC HOLIDAYS
Malaysia has numerous public holidays as a consequence of its racial profile.

January	New Year's Day
January/February	Chinese New Year (two days)
	Hindu festival of Thaipusam (in Perak, Penang, Selangor and Negeri Sembilan)
March/April	Muslim festival of Hari Raya Aidil Fitri (two days)
	Good Friday (in Sabah and Sarawak)
May	First Saturday of May: Labour Day
	6 May: Vesak Day, a time of prayer for Buddhists
	30–31 May: Pesta Menuai Harvest Festival (in Sabah)
June	1–2 June: Gawai Harvest Festival (in Sarawak)
	6 June: King's Birthday
June/July	Hari Raya Haji
	First day of Muharram.
August	31 August: National Day
August/September	Prophet Mohammed's Birthday
November	Hindu festival of Deepavali (except Sabah and Sarawak)
December	Christmas Day

If a public holiday falls at the end or beginning of a week, many Malaysians take advantage of the long weekend to have a holiday. At such times, it can be difficult to book hotel rooms or train, plane and bus tickets. Outstation taxis are often fully booked.

Furthermore, Malaysians working in urban areas traditionally return to their villages (a practice called *balik kampung*) to celebrate festivals like Chinese New Year, Hari Raya Aidil Fitri and Deepavali. Try not to travel during these *balik kampung* periods.

RADIO AND TV

Radio broadcasts exist in Malay, Mandarin, English and Tamil. There are three TV stations: two are government-owned and the third is privately run. A fourth has been planned. Major hotels have in-house video programmes.

All TV stations feature lots of popular Western programmes in English with Malay subtitles. CNN is also aired.

RELIGIOUS SERVICES

Since Malaysia is multi-racial and thus multi-religious, you will find all sorts of places of worship. Often, they are situated next to one another, as in Melaka's aptly named Harmony Street, where a mosque, Hindu temple and Chinese Taoist-Buddhist temple are located next to each other.

When visiting a mosque, try not to enter the main prayer hall. Also, refrain from visiting a mosque during prayer time (Muslims pray five times a day). Before entering a Hindu temple, remove your shoes. Churches and Chinese temples can be visited without restrictions. However, if a service is being held in a church or if prayers are held in a temple, try not to disturb the proceedings. There is no restriction on photography at places of worship, but some Muslims may not like the idea of being photographed while praying.

SHOPPING

Malaysia has embarked on a campaign to upgrade shopping facilities to compete with the popular shopping centres of Singapore and Hong Kong.

Towards this end, the government has abolished duty on several items: cigarette lighters, perfumes, skincare products, clocks and watches, ball point and fountain pens, clothes, leather goods, sportswear, cameras, pocket calculators, portable radio-cassettes, mini-computers and video cameras.

New shopping complexes in Kuala Lumpur, Penang and Johor Bahru are comparable with the best in the region in terms of building design and range of goods. But the more exciting finds (plus ambience and colour) are at the outdoor morning and night markets.

Kuala Lumpur's Jalan Petaling in Chinatown is famed as a shopping street where you can find anything you want—from exotic food to cheap watches. All large towns have morning markets and popular shopping streets. One of the best morning markets is the much-photographed and very boisterous Kota Bharu.

Note Bargaining is an integral element of shopping in Malaysia (except in department stores).

T TIME
Malaysian time is eight hours ahead of GMT. When it is 1 p.m. in Kuala Lumpur, it is 5 a.m. in London, midnight in Washington D.C. and Ottawa, and 3 p.m. in Canberra.

TIPPING
Tipping is not encouraged, though some trishaw riders, taxi drivers and tourist guides may hint that they should be rewarded. At major restaurants and hotels, a five per cent service charge is incorporated in the bill.

TOILETS
Unfortunately, Malaysian public toilets are not always the cleanest and many are in a state of disrepair.

Shopping complexes in Kuala Lumpur and major towns have started charging for usage of toilets (around M10–20 sen). These are much cleaner and tissue paper can also be bought at the counter.

Note You may not find tissue paper in public toilets. It is advisable to have a roll just in case.

TOURIST INFORMATION OFFICES
Malaysian Tourist Development Corporation offices exist in several countries:

Australia	TDC Sydney, 65 York Street, Sydney, NSW 2000. Tel: (02) 294-441. TDC Perth, 56 William Street, Perth, WA 6000. Tel: (09) 481-0400.
Canada	Malaysian Tourist Information Centre, 830 Burrard Street, Vancouver BC V622K4. Tel:(604) 689-8899.
Great Britain	57 Trafalgar Square, London WC2N 5DU. Tel: (071) 930-7932.
USA	818 West Seventh Street, Los Angeles, CA 90017. Tel: (213) 689-9702.

In **Peninsular Malaysia**, the TDC headquarters are on the 26th floor, Menara Dato Onn, Putra World Trade Centre, Jalan Tun Ismail 50480, Kuala Lumpur. Tel: (03) 293-5188.

A new Malaysian Tourist Information Centre (Matic) has opened on Jalan Ampang. This has information on all places of interest and you can also make bus, air, tour and hotel bookings there. Cultural shows are held regularly. Tel: (03) 242-3929.

In **Sabah**, the TDC office is at Block L, Lot 4, Bandaran Sinsuran, Mail Bag 136 88700, Kota Kinabalu. Tel: (088) 211-698.

In **Sarawak**, the TDC office is on the 2nd floor, AIA Building, Jalan Song Thian Cheok, 93100 Kuching. Tel: (082) 246-575,

TRAVELLING AROUND MALAYSIA

Roads are generally good except in parts of Sabah and Sarawak. The new North–South highway that links Singapore to south Thailand has made travelling by road much easier and faster.

The KTM (Keretapi Tanah Melayu) offers an efficient rail service throughout the country and fares are reasonable, too. A railway line runs the whole length of Peninsular Malaysia and links Thailand to Singapore. Another line links Gemas to Tumpat in the north-eastern state of Kelantan. In Sabah, there is a railway line that links Kota Kinabalu to Tenom. The Kuala Lumpur to Singapore service is often fully booked. If a public holiday is round the corner, it is advisable to book tickets a few days before the trip.

Taxis ply the main towns. Where the meter isn't in use, fares are usually fixed—though it is always wise to check the fare before setting off. For long distances, the normal practice is to share the taxi. Each passenger is charged a flat rate, and as soon as the driver gets four passengers, you're off. You can, however, hire the entire taxi if you so wish, in which case you will have to pay the taxi driver four times the fare.

Buses also ply the main towns. In remote places, the service is not regular and it is better to hop on to taxis.

Malaysian Airlines (MAS) and Pelangi Air operate an extensive network of domestic flights to all major towns in Malaysia, as well as to more remote places in Sabah and Sarawak.

Though a bridge now connects Penang island to the mainland, the quaint ferry service is still in operation and offers a much more colourful and enjoyable way to reach the island.

There are also regular ferry services from Lumut to the resort island of Pangkor, from Kuala Perlis and Kuala Kedah to the holiday destination of Langkawi, from Mersing to the lovely Tioman island and nearby isles, and from Kuala Besut to the Perhentian and Redang islands.

TOURS

Local tour companies offer tours around cities and the country. Some companies specialize in adventure holidays, such as trekking in the Taman Negara (the National Park), climbing Sabah's Mount Kinabalu, the highest mountain in South-East Asia, boating upriver to stay in Sarawak's longhouses, or visiting the famed Mulu and Niah Caves. Other companies organize island tours for snorkellers and divers. These firms are mostly based in Kuala Lumpur, Penang, Kuching, Kota Kinabalu and Sandakan.

W

WATER
Tap water is treated and flouridated and is safe for drinking. As a precaution drink boiled water, especially in rural areas. Mineral water can be purchased in major towns. Imported bottled mineral water can be found only in leading supermarkets.

WEIGHTS AND MEASURES
Malaysia uses the metric system.

USEFUL EXPRESSIONS

How far is it?	**Berapa jauh?**
Where?	**Dimana?**
Straight ahead	**Didepan**
Right/Left	**Kanan/Kiri**
Tonight/Evening	**Malam ini/Petang**
Morning/Noon	**Pagi/Tengah hari**
Good/Bad	**Baik/bagus Tidak baik/bagus**
Fast/Slow	**Cepat/Lambat**
Early/Late	**Awal/Lewat**
How much is it?	**Berapa harganya?**
Money/Sale	**Wang/Jualan murah**
Expensive/Cheap	**Mahal/Murah**
Thank you	**Terima kasih**
Sorry	**Minta maaf**
Hello/Goodbye	**Hello/Selamat jalan**
Welcome	**Selamat datang**
How are you?/I'm fine	**Apa khabar?/Khabar baik**
I don't understand	**Saya tidak faham**
Today/Tomorrow/Yesterday	**Hari ini/Esok/Semalam**
Please stop here	**Tolong berhenti di sini**
Let's go	**Mari kita pergi**
I'm not feeling well	**Saya rasa tidak sihat**
I need a doctor	**Saya perlu jumpa doktor**
Clean/Dirty	**Bersih/Kotor**
Water	**Air**
Train/Train station	**Keretapi/Stesyen keretapi**
Plane/Airport	**Kapal terbang/Lapangan terbang**
Hot/Cold	**Panas/Sejuk**
Beautiful	**Cantik**

NUMBERS

One	**Satu**	*Nine*	**Sembilan**
Two	**Dua**	*Ten*	**Sepuluh**
Three	**Tiga**	*Eleven*	**Sebelas**
Four	**Empat**	*Twelve*	**Duabelas**
Five	**Lima**	*Twenty*	**Duapuluh**
Six	**Enam**	*Twenty-one*	**Duapuluh satu**
Seven	**Tujuh**	*One hundred*	**Seratus**
Eight	**Lapan**	*One thousand*	**Seribu**

INDEX

Where there is more than one set of page references, the one in bold type refers to the main entry. Page references in italic refer to photographs.

029/308 SUD